Dame Elizabeth Lane

Hear
The Other Side

Audi alteram partem

Dame Elizabeth Lane

The Autobiography
of England's first Woman Judge

London
Butterworths
1985

United Kingdom	Butterworth & Co (Publishers) Ltd, 88 Kingsway, LONDON WC2B 6AB and 61A North Castle Street, EDINBURGH EH2 3LJ
Australia	Butterworths Pty Ltd, SYDNEY, MELBOURNE, BRISBANE, ADELAIDE, PERTH, CANBERRA and HOBART
Canada	Butterworth & Co (Canada) Ltd, TORONTO and VANCOUVER
New Zealand	Butterworths of New Zealand Ltd, WELLINGTON and AUCKLAND
Singapore	Butterworth & Co (Asia) Pte Ltd, SINGAPORE
South Africa	Butterworth Publishers (Pty) Ltd, DURBAN and PRETORIA
USA	Butterworth Legal Publishers, ST PAUL, Minnesota, SEATTLE, Washington, BOSTON, Massachusetts, AUSTIN, Texas and D & S Publishers, CLEARWATER, Florida

© Dame Elizabeth Lane 1985

ISBN 0 406 50240 4

Frontispiece and Backcover Photographs
by Beverley Lebarrow

Typeset by Phoenix Photosetting, Chatham
Printed and bound by Mackays of Chatham Ltd

Dedication

To the memory of my husband and son

Foreword by
The Right Honourable
The Lord Roskill, P.C.

Eheu fugaces Postume Postume, labunter anni. How true. It was on 10th May 1922 that the first woman, Miss Ivy Williams, was called to the Bar by the Inner Temple. But the opposition to the admission of women to the Bar had been long, bitter and founded on arguments which today seem laughable and sixty years ago can only have appealed to the most extreme male chauvinists. How astonished and, indeed, outraged those old men would have been could they have foreseen that only forty years on Lord Chancellor Dilhorne would appoint a woman to the County Court Bench and only three years later Lord Chancellor Gardiner would promote her to the High Court Bench. This was, indeed, Elizabeth Lane's triumph in a profession still twenty years ago male dominated. And this last appointment came only twenty-five years after she had been called to the Bar also by the Inner Temple at the age of thirty-five, an age at which today many contemplate and some achieve taking silk.

Thus and in other ways too Elizabeth Lane blazed a trail which many have since been able to follow, some perhaps unconscious how much their freedom within the profession and their own professional successes have owed to her initiative and courage forty-five years ago.

Hers is a tale which should be told. Characteristically she tells it with brevity and modesty, recording her tragedies along with her triumphs.

I have had the good fortune to enjoy her friendship for many years. She has now seriously put that friendship at risk by asking me to write this foreword to her story. But our friendship can, I hope, withstand even that strain and I am delighted to do so. I am sure others will enjoy her story as I have done.

The Lord Roskill, P.C.

HOUSE OF LORDS
October 1985

Preface

There are two reasons for my choice of a Latin legal maxim as a title: firstly it expresses the duty of all those who exercise judicial functions and epitomises the requirement of impartiality and equal treatment of all those who come before the courts, be they high or low, rich and powerful or poor and weak.

Secondly and much less loftily, outside the circle of my relatives and friends I have mainly been known as a wigged and gowned barrister or a wigged and robed judge. I therefore hope that it will be of interest to read the inside story of my background and life before and after, somewhat belatedly, I became a member of the Bar and later of the previously masculine Judiciary of England. For judicial purposes England includes Wales, which provides some of our judges.

Elizabeth Lane.

Acknowledgments

I gratefully acknowledge the kindly encouragement, not to say nagging, of my brother Lindsay and my friend Mrs Gwenllyan Davies which finally resulted in my writing this book. I am also grateful to Mrs Molly Izzard for her skilled advice which I happily heeded.

Contents

Contents

Chapter 1
Forebears

The discussion as to the relative importance of heredity and environment in the development of human beings goes on endlessly. Physical characteristics may often be traceable to one's forebears, though who is to say why a strain of stalwarts may produce a weakling and vice versa? I find difficulty in accepting the theory that juvenile or adult misdeeds are unerringly attributable to what occurred in early life. No doubt this can be so in some cases but the theory leaves unexplained the considerable number of stable and happy childhoods followed by thoroughly unsatisfactory lives or the, perhaps smaller, numbers of deprived and unhappy children who turn into admirable and successful adults. Perhaps the right explanation is that each of us is unique and that although we are born with certain predispositions and are subject to various influences, it is essentially what we make of ourselves which governs what we become: we are our own responsibility. It seems to me that religious belief is the greatest guide and help in becoming the satisfactory person each of us is innately capable of being.

However that may be, a happy childhood must be a great initial advantage in life; so is a good physique. I was blessed with both.

Warriors – a judge (Irish) – a poet and some artists

So far as my own ancestry is concerned, according to an English translation of a Latin genealogy of my mother's family, her first known forebear was "Le Seigneur Homo de Valenscourt or Wallcourt (according to Guillaume de Tuillier the famous Norman chronologer)". He was a successful Marshal in the army of William the Conqueror at the Battle of Hastings. The Seigneur was rewarded and in 1070 "was possessed of five Manors or Lordships in Suffolk and three in Kent". In 1172 two grandsons of his, Humphrey and Homo, distinguished themselves as Knights Banneret in the army which King Henry II led into Ireland. At a date given as 1175, but which should probably be 1185, Earl John, King Henry's second son, as Governor of Ireland, granted two baronies in the County of Limerick to Humphrey and his heirs male for ever at 20 Knights' fees. Homo also received "considerable possessions" in the province of Leinster and in 1197 was Lord Justice of Ireland. So far as I know, he was the only previous judicial member of the family.

The whole family was, of course, staunchly Roman Catholic and its members appear to have taken part in just about every war, or factional fight with which Ireland was, and still is, chronically cursed. In the reign of Queen Elizabeth I, the family properties were confiscated and given to her nominees. Nevertheless, either she or King James I acceded to a Petition to the Throne by some of the Chiefs of the Province of Munster and "taking their distressed condition into Royal Consideration restored some in full and some in part to their ancient inheritances and possessions". Richard Wall or de Wallcourt "only got a grant of his family seat of Dunmoylan and 15 plow lands adjacent thereto which he enjoyed in peace until the latter end of Cromwell the Regicide's Usurpation – who sent one Oliver Stephens into this Kingdom with a grant of whatever Estate he might take a liking to therein". He chose Dunmoylan and "forcibly possessed himself thereof . . . and in order to secure it more effectively he caused the said Richard Wall or de Wallcourt to be beheaded at his castle gate under pretence that he favoured the Duke of Lemir's design of being Protector of Ireland". Richard was a poet and a wit; at the time of his death he was over a hundred years old and completely blind and "being ordered by his murderer to fix his head upon the block he told him he might do it himself as he could see to do it".

So far as I know, poor Richard was the only poet the family produced. There were a number of artists, the only one of whom was well known in this country was Charles Allen du Val. He was born in 1810 (1808 according to the National Biographical Dictionary), the son of Edward Octavius du Val who had married the daughter of the Danish Consul General for Ireland. It was Charles Allen who left Ireland for England and married an Englishwoman. One of their numerous children was my maternal grandmother. She married an Englishman.

Landed gentry – a move south – in commerce – an unusual death

Less information is available to me about my father's early ancestry. His family name was Coulborn. According to my elder brother's researches carried out before he died in 1968, a forebear was Warden of the Forest of Delamere in Cheshire in the reign of one of the Henry's; I cannot remember which one. I gather that this was a post with considerable perks such as disposing of timber and game. One branch of the family lived in Scotland on the banks of the Clyde. The family story was that because the wife was always ailing, the doctor's advice was accepted that she should be taken to live in the south, preferably at Brighton. She and her husband travelled by sea. When the ship put into Liverpool they saw New Brighton on the other side of the Mersey, liked the look of it, disembarked and went to live there, perhaps in the mistaken belief that the similarity of the name betokened similarity in other ways, including climate.

Later there was a move inland to Timperley, then a rural area. The family land marched with that of a family named Rushton. There was a village of that name, which I gather no longer exists as such, although in the 1960s at any rate there was a farm bearing the name, the owner of which had erected the disused road sign to Rushton at the entrance to the farm. A Coulborn son married a Miss Rushton who was heiress to the estate, thus uniting the two properties very satisfactorily. The name 'Rushton' has been used as a Christian name in the family since then and was one of my elder brother's names.

Nevertheless the call of the banks of the Mersey seems to have been strong and I know from official records that my great grandfather and his two unmarried brothers lived in New Brighton from the 1860s until they all three died within a few days of each other in early 1895 from influenza, of which there was then an epidemic. In the earlier records my great grandfather was described as a grain merchant. Later all three brothers including the youngest, who was a civil engineer, owned the ferries which plied between Liverpool and the Wirral. Later still they sold the ferries whereafter they were officially described as 'gentlemen'. The paddleboat ferries included the "Iris" and the "Daffodil" both of which were used in the raid on Zeebrugge in the First World War. The former was deliberately sunk as a blockship; the latter returned to her duties on the Mersey, renamed the "Royal Daffodil" in recognition of her war service. I crossed the river in her more than once as a child.

The Scottish ancestry was recognised in my grandfather's Christian names of William Wallace and my father and elder brother were educated at Fettes College, Edinburgh, where they had the same headmaster at the beginning and end of his tenure of the post. My younger brother was destined to go there too, but my mother rebelled because he had been a delicate child whom she thought unfitted for the Spartan conditions at Fettes. Despite opposition, she made arrangements for him to go to Westminster instead.

My grandfather and his two sons were interested in sports. Grandpa and my father's brother Ernest were both good shots and Bisley cup winners. Grandpa, who was in the Militia, gave an exhibition of shooting before Queen Victoria at her Golden Jubilee celebrations. Ernest was also a hockey player and at one time goalkeeper for England. Father held (jointly) the public schools' long jump record.

Grandpa married a Welshwoman, Maria Armstrong of Ruthin. She was a very prim person, curiously lacking in a sense of humour. Presented with a copy of *Alice in Wonderland* and invited to comment on it, she said that she thought it "highly improbable". As I remember her, her general attitude to life was one of disapproval. Oddly, her son Ernest was known as a wit. An air of Victorian dignified imperturbility was maintained in their house. On one occasion Grandma returned home and smelled burning. She found Grandpa sitting reading his newspaper. His response to her expressed alarm was "Yes, my dear, the kitchen is on fire but calm yourself, the brigade has been sent for." When we went to stay in the house and made Grandma's companion laugh, the laugh had a rusty sound, so my mother said.

Grandma had a sister of very different calibre. As a widow in her seventies, she continued to live in the large family house to which her children and grandchildren frequently returned. About 1.00 a m one night in about the year 1913 she heard noises coming from downstairs. There were servants in the house and a bell-pull by her bed, but she elected to put on a wrap and to investigate herself. In the dining-room she found some of her grand-children and their friends having a late supper-party and consuming lobster and (her) champagne. After protest-ing that she should have been notified beforehand, she sat down and shared the repast. In the morning she was unwell and was convinced that there had been "something wrong with the lobster". Unfortunately her doctor was away and a young locum attended. He suggested that perhaps lobster and champagne in the middle of the night were "not very wise at our age." She was furious and ordered him out of her room. Shortly afterwards, in order to prove her point, she had lobster and champagne brought to her bedroom at 1.00 a m. She consumed them with relish and the following morning was down to breakfast, as usual at 8 o'clock. The young did give another supper party and duly invited her. She presided, decked out in her diamonds. When someone went to call her the next morning she was found to be dead.

Her executors were directed to have her taken to her grave in a motor-hearse (a novelty in those days), which was to drive as fast as possible. I was considered too young to go to the funeral but I remember my grandmother's chauffeur saying to me afterwards, "It was downright disgusting, the hearse went so fast I couldn't keep up with it in your grandmother's car." It is good not to go out with a whimper.

So much, too much perhaps, for family history and tales. It is plain that I am of very mixed ancestry, English, Welsh, Irish, French with perhaps a few drops of Danish blood. A hybrid indeed.

Chapter 2

Childhood, schooling and growing-up

Early days in peacetime

I was born on 9 August 1905, with a brother, Rushton, four years older than myself, and a younger brother, Lindsay, to follow four years later.

It was a good time to be born: a stable Edwardian era with settled values and yet with great and rapid changes to come in a very inventive period. People of my age have seen (and heard) the coming into use of the telephone, the motor car and the aeroplane, not to mention radio, television and the micro-chip. We are old enough to remember both World Wars. We must have witnessed the greatest social changes, world-wide, of any period of equal length in history.

Socially, I suppose that our family could be categorised as upper middle class, and neither rich nor poor. As children, my brothers and I were loved and very well cared for, with that invaluable feeling of security, unrecognised as such until one looks back and realises how fortunate one was. We were brought up in the Christian faith, which was another blessing: it seems to me to be more difficult to bring up children satisfactorily without an appeal to Higher Authority. No doubt religious upbringing and practice in Victorian times often contained a good deal of hypocrisy and some of the 'pi' children it produced were horrid little prigs by our standards, but we escaped that sort of atmosphere as religious teaching grew wiser and more honest.

One of the most important people in one's life when I was young was one's nanny. Occasionally we used to be shocked by what other children told us of how their nannies treated them; ours was unfailingly kind and comforting but believed in discipline. She was not a trained nanny, far from it. What happened was that in the hands of my first nurse who was, I think, the midwife and referred to as 'the monthly', I cried very loudly whenever I was being dressed or undressed and particularly while being bathed. On one occasion Mother, hearing even louder screams than usual discovered that I had just been put into much too hot a bath and had emerged, so she said, looking like a boiled lobster. Afterwards a young housemaid called Mary Wass, with obvious embarrassment at her own temerity, asked if she might bath the baby. Mother enquired what she could know about bathing babies; the answer was that she was eldest of a large family and had been bathing successive babies for years. She was allowed to try her hand on me. For the first time I did not cry. That was how she started as nanny. Not that we called her "Nanny". Mother said that that was an undignified way in which to address anyone and that we were to call her by her beautiful name of Mary. Similarly, we were not allowed to call Mother "Mummy", that again was regarded as undignified whereas Mother was a beautiful name. Perhaps illogically, "Daddy" was allowed. We got out of the difficulty by the use of nick-names, some of which anyway were not forbidden. Mary became "Wagger" because in night attire she wore her hair in a long plait which wagged from side to side as she walked.

As her first infant charge, I was always Wagger's favourite of the three of us. I was wholly unconscious of this until Mother mentioned it to me when I was nearly grown-up and then I realised that it had been so.

It was not very long before Mother's confidence in Wagger was sufficiently strong for us to be left in her charge, subject to remote control by an aunt, while the parents went away on what must have been most interesting holidays to St Petersburg, Prague, Buda-Pest, Vienna, Madeira and so on. Years later Mother told me that her favourites were St Petersburg and Vienna because of the wonderful balls and the splendid uniforms. I think that my Father's favourite holiday was cruising.

As a child one of my abiding interests was always babies. Dolls were quite a good substitute but I remember when I was four years old the enormous joy of finding that I had a baby brother. I vividly recall the first time I was allowed to hold him, sitting with my legs outstretched on the nursery floor so that if I dropped him (which of course I did not) he would not have far to fall. He was a delightful child and I happily retain my affectionate relationship with him to this day.

At the time of my earliest recollections we lived at Bowdon in Cheshire. My Father had an allowance from his father (quite a usual arrangement in those days) but decided to go into business and chose the then prosperous cotton trade. He became the owner or joint owner of a mill at Bury in Lancashire, a reasonable distance away. The house had a big garden which I loved. Mother believed in letting small children run free. A large handbell was rung to summon us back to the house, but sometimes personal search was necessary. I feel so sorry for children brought up in flats.

One of my treats when I was six or seven years old was for Mother to take me with her when she went shopping. My favourite destination was a cake shop called Meng and Ecker's, where I was always presented with a glass of milk and a sponge cake, for which I am sure that my mother was not asked to pay. Shopkeepers were apt to do this sort of thing in those days. The grocer usually had a delicious biscuit handy. But the best shop of all was Jackson's, the toy shop. Besides more expensive items, there were two large tables, one spread with penny toys

9

and the other with twopenny ones. I was given a Saturday penny in those days (you had to be quite big before you got sixpence, let alone a shilling). It was an agonising choice: should I have a penny toy or go without until next week and have a twopenny one? I think that I usually had a penny one.

If some kind grown-up gave us a florin or half-a-crown it had to go into the money-box which could only be opened by Wagger or a parent. Anyway at the age of about ten out of the money-box I was easily able to pay for my first bicycle bought from a friend who had outgrown it. The price was five shillings. The Post Office Savings account, into which regular payments were made by grandparents, was inviolable.

Children's parties were great fun in those days and I still retain my liking for jellies. In common with a lot of other little girls, over my party dress I wore a little Red Riding Hood cloak on the way there and back. The moment when the nannies arrived to collect their charges always came too soon. There were often searching questions asked after a party as to how much one had had to eat (it was compulsory to refuse an offered third helping), had one remembered to say thank you to the hostess and so forth. Certainly my generation was taught early in life the elements of good manners.

For pets we had cats, rabbits and mice. I did not really like picking up a rabbit by its ears as I had been taught to do and managed to slip a hand under its dangling back legs.

By modern standards, our playthings were simple. We had some clockwork toys but mainly we made our own amusements with things such as a rocking horse, a pedal car, building bricks, balls and the like. In my case there was a doll's house and a number of dolls with their cots and prams. The boys of course had trains and lead soldiers, but I seem to remember that the railway lines had a maddening way of coming apart, that the trains fell over all too frequently and that lead soldiers had an irritating habit of losing their heads. The garden was perhaps the best place to play. I always contrived to get myself grubby there (one of my Mother's friends used to refer to me as "dear dirty little Betty".) It is a habit which persists. Even now if I am gardening, I contrive to move off the kneeling mat and despite wearing gloves my fingers manage to get earthy.

If I have unwittingly given the impression that I was a 'good' child, this is erroneous. I was not. Mother said that I was the only one of her children who was naughty for the sake of being naughty.

It was Mother's view that children should not start to have lessons until they were about seven years old. (There was then no unkind Act of Parliament providing for schooling to commence at the tender age of five.) Mother herself started me on the path of learning to read and write. I loathed pothooks but I was very keen to learn to read so that I need no longer be dependent on grown-ups reading to me. I might say that I took to *The Cat sat on the Mat* (illustrated) like a duck to water. I still preserve a few of my childhood books. *Hoodie, The Cuckoo Clock* and *The Tapestry Room* by Mrs Molesworth and also *The Rose Book for Girls* were my favourites. One might think that the modern child would find such books intolerably boring, but this is not necessarily so. Recently I have lent all those I have mentioned to several little girls who have loved them. We had Grimms' and Hans Andersen's Fairy Tales. Latterly I heard of a complaint that those of Grimm were too frightening for young children: a mistaken view I think. Children, happy ones at any rate, seem to me too assimilate horrifying stories very easily and to enjoy them when they are recognisably unreal.

The modern child, accustomed to watching television programmes, often not just those intended for young eyes, cannot know the real excitement of going to the theatre, as did a child of the magic lantern age. I have vivid recollections of my first visit to a theatre when I was six or seven years old. We were to go to a pantomime in

Manchester, in which incidentally George Robey was appearing. It was snowing during the day and I was told that if the snow became too thick we could not go. The agony of standing, nose glued to the window pane watching the snowflakes! I insisted on putting on my party dress in the middle of the afternoon although we were not to leave until early evening, convinced that if I were ready it would make it more likely that we should go. And we did. But the parents decided that we should have to leave before the performance ended. Wagger whispered in my ear that we were going: I did not hear her: she shook me: I did not feel it. Fortunately we were occupying a box and I had to be picked up bodily and carried out. It was only then that I realised what was happening and gave a shriek which echoed through the theatre. Perhaps a child's capacity for being absorbed is not always recognised. An unheeded instruction to leave whatever it may be is not necessarily deliberate disobedience. The instruction may be heard but it may not penetrate the conscious mind immediately. I do not mean that one should expect to repeat every instruction but only to recognise that sometimes the absorption is very deep.

Similarly not all adults appreciate a child's capacity to suffer grief. I shall never forget the searing sorrow, the utter heart-break, I felt when just about the time of my eighth birthday Mother told me that Wagger was leaving us. Rushton had been away at prep school for years and Lindsay and I were old enough for a nursery governess. Mother said that she had engaged a very nice young governess whom we should like very much. My retort was that I should hate her. It was nearly bedtime when the news was imparted, no doubt because it was thought that I should soon be asleep and would feel better about it in the morning. That was a mistaken view. I crawled down inside the bedclothes to the bottom of the bed, screwed myself into the smallest ball I could and wept bitterly for a very long time. It was not much better in the morning. Some time after Wagger left us she married and

12

had children of her own and I am sure that she made a wonderfully good mother.

I think that an interval was allowed to elapse between Wagger's departure and the arrival of the governess. I remember holding Lindsay's hand as we were pushed into the room where she was waiting to meet us alone. I have no doubt that we were both polite but I felt a deep resentment towards her. Lindsay took to her quite shortly after her arrival and it was not very long before I did so too and we both became very fond of her. Her name was Florence Margaret Wild and some years after she left us she became the much loved headmistress of a girls' school. Lindsay was always her favourite, a fact I recognised at the time if only because if anything involving the pair of us went wrong it was always held to be my fault – very justly most of the time, but not quite always. It is remarkable how children recognise and resent injustice.

We left Bowdon when I was about eight years old. Father had been far from sucessful as a business man. I gather that he lost much more money than he made. Worse still, he lost his health and those delightful games he used to play with us came to an end. I think that he probably had a stroke though the cause of his trouble was never diagnosed to Mother's satisfaction. The parents heard of a Swiss doctor with a reputation for treating such patients as my father with his somewhat restricted bodily movements. So the house was sold and Mother and Father went to Montreux. Governess and young were deposited with grandparents. Sometime later it was decided to let Miss Wild, who had never been out of England before, bring Lindsay and myself to Switzerland. The journey involved spending a night in a Paris hotel. We made it safely if not altogether unadventurously. The parents were staying in an hotel in Montreux but Miss Wild, Lindsay and I were parked in a pension run by two English ladies, Miss Glennie and Miss Bond, and taken every morning to visit the parents and to eat one of

13

those gorgeous Swiss cream cakes at the nearby Kursaal. It was not until 1968 that I revisited Montreux and then was astonished at how well I remembered it, even that plank bridge over an inlet of the lake which was still there 55 years after I had been so frightened to cross it.

At Christmas 1913 we went to Zweisimmen for the winter sports – a joyful revelation to the young. Father could not take much part in the sports but did manage to do some skating and also to indulge his hobby of photography. When the spring came we went to Glion and how lovely and unforgettable the spring flowers were, scented golden fields of cowslips and dazzling blue gentians for which we searched on our walks. Recently I returned to Glion in the spring and searched for the flowering fields, but found none.

Wartime

Rumours of war brought us back to England in 1914. When it started we were staying with my mother's mother in the charming house she had herself designed and had built in a shopless place on the Sussex coast later called Angmering-on-Sea. In 1915 we went to live in a house belonging to a bachelor friend of the parents, Eustace Harrison, at Burton Point in the Wirral. He had rejoined the cavalry and departed with his horse to France. We took over the house with its large staff of servants. The grounds covered 13 acres. There were cows to supply the house and the estate cottages with milk and butter. Better still there was a horse for me to ride. My father wished me to ride side-saddle as my mother had done, but she persuaded him to let me have my own way and ride astride. Perhaps I inherited my love of riding from my mother who had been a most intrepid horsewoman. On one occasion, before her marriage, she decided to see if her mother's carriage horses could be persuaded to jump. They could. The trouble

14

that they gave afterwards when harnessed to the carriage led to discovery of the cause. Father told me of how Mother's riding exploits had terrified him during their engagement. I do not think that she ever rode after their marriage. Her other great interest was in music. She had studied at the Royal Academy of Music and become such an accomplished pianist that had she lived in a later age she would probably have become a professional concert pianist. But in those days the idea of a gentlewoman performing on a public platform did not meet with approval. I believe that when Irene and Violet Vanburgh went on the stage it caused a great scandal. Father had quite a good baritone voice and we children were brought up to love music. But I was the only one taught to play an instrument, the piano. At one stage Mother tried to teach me. She was always kind about my efforts but I knew what a disappointment my playing must be to her, even though over the years I attained a reasonable competence and loved playing. I was so conscious of my shortcoming that later when I was at school I was allowed to give up piano lessons and have singing lessons instead. Today I cannot play a note on the piano and, although I sing in Church now, it is an act of faith rather than a contribution to the music.

During the First World War, children as well as adults were inculcated with hatred of the Germans. It was made inevitable for me to be filled with hatred when a very dear cousin was killed in France in 1916. I remember with some surprise now what blood-thirsty stories we were told and read about "the Hun". This was of lasting effect and the forgiving spirit which I had been trying to cultivate between the World Wars took a nasty knock when the second one came. I am trying again and perhaps it is easier now that I am old. Like a lot of other people I could not work up any real animosity towards the Italians in the last war and I have happily returned to Italy and Italian friends on numerous occasions since the war ended.

Before the first war ended we left Colonel Harrison's house and went to live in the depths of the Shropshire countryside in a village called Weston-under-Redcastle. The house was on the edge of Hawkestone Park and we had the run of the park with a private gate into it. It was so large that one could get well away from the sound of the schoolroom bell and even personal search could fail to find one. A splendid feeling it was, even though one might be in trouble afterwards for not knowing that it had been time to come indoors. The house was without gas or electricity, cooking was done on a coalburning range and water had to be pumped into the house from a well. A lamplit room had a charm which, thank goodness, we are spared today.

He must have been about 40 years old when my father disregarded his doctor's advice and joined the army. This would have been about the year 1917 when no doubt the physical fitness standards for enlistment had been substantially reduced because of the appalling number of war casualties. He was transferred to what was then the Royal Flying Corps but not to flying duties. At one stage he was posted to Ireland and came home on leave bringing with him a large suitcase at which Mother exclaimed in horror because it was made of fibre and not of leather, as all luggage should have been. But all was well when she saw the contents, butter, ducks ready for roasting and all manner of rarities under the quite severe rationing we had in that war as well as in the last one.

At the age of about 11 I was considered to be quite old enough to do war-work. This took the form of being responsible for the sitting hens. I had to keep a sharp eye open for any hen which appeared to be going broody and choose the right moment to sit her. There was a splendidly maternal Rhode Island Red with a most creditable chicken output record until one morning when I found her out of the nest and dead. No doubt she had been attacked by a rat. The eggs were almost cold. No other hen was broody except for a White Leghorn and I was assured that she could not be used because the breed was never sufficiently stable for the purpose. Needs must! She hatched out two of the clutch, one of which was fine and the other bald and weak. I was told that it would be impossible to rear the latter, but with patience born of obstinacy, I fed it by hand for weeks and in the end its feathers grew and it became one of the best layers in the flock. How satisfying, if rare, it was to prove the grown-ups wrong. There was a large lake in the park with fish in it. In Father's absence I was allowed to take one of his rods and see what I could catch. I came home in triumph with several fish. What they were I cannot say, but when they were cooked they tasted of nothing but mud. Undaunted, I helped myself to several of the rods, stuck them in the banks at intervals and frequently caught supplies of fish to be cooked as hen-food.

Despite the fact that our nickname for Miss Wild was "Wisdoms", when I was about 11 or 12, she told Mother that she was no longer competent to teach me as my age required. The first expedient tried was to press the local curate into service as a tutor. Poor man! He was a bachelor and more accustomed to visiting elderly parishioners than to dealing with the young. My French was much better than his, but he was at home with algebra, geometry and Latin, of which I knew nothing. We were both glad when the arrangement ended.

Peace again – schooldays – and a return to school

In order to soften the blow of being sent to boarding school straight away (girls were not expected to be as tough as little boys who were packed off to prep school at the age of about seven or eight), it was arranged that I should stay with a friend, Lorimer Rome, in the Wirral, and share her governess for a couple of terms. It was a very happy arrangement for me and the Romes were kindness itself. I do not remember being homesick at all.

But it was a different story when I did go to boarding school soon after my thirteenth birthday. I was horribly homesick and it was an alien place to me for weeks on end. I was in my first term there when the war ended and I was so joyfully excited that for some time I could hardly think of anything else. It was a very small school called 'Twizzletwig' at Hindhead and, no doubt very understandably, the headmistress took a dislike to me and always seemed ready to pounce. After I had been there for a year the headmistress died: for me it was a battle between my conscience, which told me that it was wicked to rejoice at her death, and a strong desire to do so. She was succeeded by the assistant headmistress, Miss Humphreys, and a sister of hers. They were kind and life was happy again. My greatest friend at that school was Patricia, daughter of Edgar Wallace, whose books I loved. I think that we quarrelled in the end, but not until after I had spent a most exciting few days at her London home in Clarence Gate Gardens. Mother can hardly have appreciated what the ménage was or I should not have been allowed to go. But while there I found nothing strange in the absence of Mrs Wallace or the presence of the charming female secretary.

Part of another school holiday was spent in very different surroundings. Miss Wild at the time was in the Church Army in London, trying to fulfil a pledge made by her father to the Almighty that if his sick wife recovered from an illness, as she did, he would dedicate one of his three daughters to the service of the Church. I did not have to be grown-up to conclude that this was a monstrous thing to do. Miss Wild reckoned that three years' service would suffice. She must have had time off-duty while I was staying with her in a hostel in the area of Harrow Road for she took me to all sorts of interesting and exciting places and entertainments, including a performance of 'Monsieur Beaucaire'. We attended a Sunday morning service in the Temple Church, sitting in the high-backed pews in which a child disappeared from view when sitting or kneeling down. Those pews lasted until the German Air Force destroyed them in the last war. Thereafter Temple-dwellers attended services at St Dunstan's-in-the-West until the Temple church was restored, with pews having all-round visibility. Miss Wild did perform some of her duties while I was staying with her and, for me, it was a most exalting experience to be left in charge of a Church Army shop selling second-hand clothes. A pair of socks might cost a penny and a child's dress perhaps sixpence or a shilling. I do not think that Mother realised how much I should see and hear of the seamy side of life, but I am sure that it did me no harm: quite the contrary. I developed then and still have great admiration for the work of the Church Army.

When I was 15 I went to Malvern Girls' College, for the first two years in Middle School in a house called 'The Benhams', and for the final year in Senior House. When I first went there I was much too bumptious. At Twizzlet-wig I had done well in class work and at the only two games we played, netball and tennis. It was a very salu-tary experience to be one of a large number with plenty of girls who were much better than I was in both spheres of activity. However, it was not long before I settled down and I thoroughly enjoyed my time at Malvern. We played hockey and lacrosse in the winter, although I soon gave up the latter, and tennis in the summer. There was also cricket for those who wished to play. I never did. We had our own swimming bath which was a great joy. But best of all was hockey. I loved it. Indeed it was my main interest in life and I could hardly wait for classroom periods to end so that we could get back to the hockey pitch. I was not the studious kind. Such interest as I managed to muster was in English, history and botany. Latin bored me to death although later in life I was glad to have at least an elementary knowledge of it, nearly all of which I have now forgotten. Having failed to concen-trate on my class work during most of the term, when exam time was near something like panic set in and I really worked hard at revision. Many a night after lights-out I retired down the bedclothes with a torch in order to 'swot' unseen. Perhaps in so doing I unwittingly trained my memory for the rapid absorption of facts involved in reading a barrister's brief, facts which one could forget when the case was over. Anyway I never failed any of my exams and at 16 got through the 'Higher Oxford' which carried an exemption from 'Matric'. When I was to move into Senior House at the age of 17 the question was whether it should be the sixth form and reading for Oxford or Cambridge, as the headmistress recommended, or something else. My own views, which were allowed to prevail, were very definite: when my final year at school would end just before my eighteenth birthday I should have done with academics and have a good time. The idea of university and unremitting scholastic endeavour did not appeal at all. Meanwhile what of the intervening year? I had to think hard of some reason to avoid the sixth form so I developed an ambition to go into journalism, for which a year in the College Secretarial Department would be invaluable. (It had a good hockey team.) The parental view was, I think, that higher education for women was unnecessary and that I should probably marry when quite young as in fact I did. I have no regrets about never having been to university. Times have changed since then and I recognise that it is virtually essential now for women to go to university if they wish to enter any of the learned professions or embark on many other ways of earning a living. They have my sympathy! I cannot say that I took kindly to shorthand or typing or even made any real use of them. Not having used a typewriter for many years before I retired I find now that I am an execrable typist and my mistakes are legion. As I dislike trying to rub out my errors I usually type a capital X through them and start the word again. There often has to be a P.S. apologising for the typing – handwritten.

I did not believe it when I was told by adults that

schooldays were the happiest days of one's life, but certainly I was very happy at Malvern.

It must have been about 20 years after I left Malvern when I saw in a court building my old games' mistress, Miss Balsillie. It was easy for me to recall her name, what was remarkable was that she immediately remembered mine. Seeing me in barrister's robes she shook her head sadly and said, "I always thought you were one of us". So I was.

Some 56 years after leaving Malvern I returned there as principal guest and speaker for an Annual Speech-Day and Prize-Giving. I was somewhat apprehensive as to whether what I wished to say would be well received. Happily, it was. I had always preserved my Senior House blazer and at the end of my speech I produced it from the bag, in which it had been hidden, as tangible proof of my affectionate loyalty to the school. That went down very well. I stayed the weekend in that holy of holies, the headmistress's flat in the College building. Old habits die hard and old associations tend to revive them: I had to keep reminding myself not to answer the headmistress with a respectful "Yes, Miss Owen", "No, Miss Owen".

Great improvements and large additions had been made to the school since my day, which impressed me very much. So did a concert given by the school orchestra and some soloists. It almost made me blush to remember the concerts of that earlier time which can hardly have been admired, except perhaps by fond parents.

Before I left school our parents, Lindsay and I went to Chamonix. There I met a dashing young Parisian with his weathy widowed mother who seemed to me to be something of a dragoness. She clearly did not like Pierre's interest in me and my mother most certainly did not like mine in him. He and I corresponded faithfully for over a year after we went our separate ways. He came to England to see me, but missed me because we were away from where he expected to find me. I do not think that either of us really regarded marriage to each other as a practicable or even desirable proposition. In the end I told Mother so, but nothing would convince her that I would not become the wife of a foreigner who would probably have mistresses, with a disapproving mother-in-law who would hold the purse strings. It was largely to save me from such a fate that it was decided just after my nineteenth birthday that I should go to stay with my elder brother in Canada. I was more than willing to go, Pierre had lasted longer than any of my other young men and enough was enough.

Grown-up and to Canada – Randall

Brother Rushton at that time had a flat at Westmount, Montreal. After starting out to be a marine engineer he decided that his real interest in life was history so he switched courses and was reading for a history degree at McGill University. He was also doing coaching work to supplement his allowance. He met me when my ship' docked very early in the morning. After a brief greeting he asked, "Can you cook?" As I did not even know how to boil an egg, my response was, "No, but I can learn." The next day I bought a copy of Mrs Beeton. I stayed with Rushton for a year. He had been neglecting his meals before I arrived but thereafter put on two stone in weight so I cannot have done too badly. He was very liberal with hospitality to some of his university friends: several rather hungry young men used to ask if they could have an English pudding. Suet or sponge puddings seemed to be an unknown quantity in Canada. The standard sweet was ice-cream. What really defeated my culinary efforts was the making of gravy. I realised that it could not have occurred to Mother that Rushton did not have proper domestic arrangements but I decided to tell her that I was doing the cooking and to ask for the secret of gravy making. Her response was to send a cable

saying, "Have sent a draft to Bank. Get servant at once."
As we later confessed to Mother, we did nothing of the
sort. With the unexpected windfall we went ski-ing in
the Laurentian mountains. We stayed in a wooden hotel
run by a Red Indian. He could only count up to ten, so the
hotel guests had to make out their own bills. There was
no water laid on and the only heating was from a furnace
which discharged hot air through two large grids in the
floor of the lounge. With outside temperatures sometimes 20° or more below freezing, when the guests came
in from ski-ing they all stood huddled tightly together on
the grids. It was no use having any water in the unheated
bedrooms: it would have frozen solid and hot water had
to be brought round in jugs left outside bedroom doors
every morning. I cannot remember really suffering from
the cold, even dressing or undressing, although Rushton
had the horrible pain of a frozen big toe on one occasion.

Judged by English standards of those days Montreal in
1924–5 was a somewhat lawless place. There were many
hold-ups, for example, people in a dance-hall who were
lined up by gunmen and robbed of money and jewellery,
also many individual cases of what we should now call
'mugging'. One friend of Rushton's was robbed and
thrown over a fence into a field where he lay for more
than 24 hours in freezing snow and afterwards surprised
everyone by recovering. I do not, however, recall any
attacks on elderly women. Like many other men
Rushton carried a revolver when he went out at night and
I was never allowed to go out alone after dark, although
the streets were mainly well-lit. When we moved to
another apartment which was on the ground floor and I
had my bedroom window open in hot weather, Rushton
gave me a revolver (I had earlier been taught how to use
one) and told me to sleep with it under my pillow. One
night I was woken by something landing on top of me
but I never even thought of the revolver, which was
perhaps as well because it turned out to be nothing worse
than a very large cat.

A considerable proportion of the Montreal population was French Canadian, many of whom did not make very happy citizens: they were still resentful towards France for having lost the colony in the eighteenth century but felt little or no loyalty to the English conquerors. Many were bi-lingual which the English Canadians were not, so police officers, postmen and other officials who came in contact with the public had to be mainly French Canadians. In the countryside of Quebec Province some of the inhabitants still spoke the out-of-date French their forebears had spoken in France, but in Montreal, at any rate, this had been considerably debased. A plumber who came to mend a radiator announced the completion of "le job" in words which, spelt phonetically, sounded as "Say fay le rajter." An aristocratic Frenchman who visited Montreal told us angrily that the locals did not speak French and that he could not understand a word they said.

While I was there a French Canadian police chief was convicted of taking bribes mainly, if I remember aright, in connection with drinking regulations and brothels. To my astonishment instead of being sent to prison he was fined and re-instated. Rushton said that he was otherwise efficient and that anyone else appointed in his place would probably do the same.

The police carried arms and I recall the horror of an occasion when they shot dead a fleeing suspect as he tried to climb a railing in a crowded street. A much less harrowing and rather exciting occasion was when I saw two splendid looking 'Mounties' go to a house where they arrested a wanted man. He offered no resistance. There was one spectacle of a very different and thrilling kind which I shall never forget: after midnight in the depth of winter, the main street deserted of traffic, long high walls of banked-up snow separating the sidewalks from the roadway, and along dashed a scarlet fire engine, the men's helmets and the big, clanging brass bell gleaming in the lamplight, drawn by white horses at full gallop.

No doubt nowadays things are very different in

24

Montreal, but I have only been back there twice since 1925 and then too briefly to form any real impression save from huge new buildings which had so altered the place that I could hardly recognise it and could not find my way about.

I hope and believe that the anti-English feeling is less wide-spread now. Certainly the French Canadian soldiers with whom I came in contact during the last war had no trace of it – they were Canadian and that was that. And I believe that they fought very bravely.

When I joined him in Canada Rushton was always talking about a friend of his, Randall Lane, an Englishman who had been working in Canada but was away in Italy pursuing his interest in Italian art and literature. According to Rushton, he was a most remarkable man with a brilliant intellect, a wide culture and a sparkling wit – a paragon it seemed. I got very tired of hearing about him and thought that if I met him I should dislike him. So I was not at all pleased when I heard that he was returning to Canada and coming to stay with us. He arrived with very little warning on the morning of Christmas Eve 1924. I had provided a hot-pot for lunch, which fortunately was enough for three people and happened to be about the best one I have ever made. Rushton had an engagement for that evening, which left me, still secretly hostile, to entertain Randall. Perhaps because he viewed the prospect with no greater enthusiasm that I did, he asked Rushton if he could take me to the theatre. The play we saw was called 'Everything One Dollar' and was largely concerned with the sale of boxes of chocolates. Randall was much chagrined to find that the theatre had run out of boxes of chocolates so that all he could offer me was a 5-cent packet of Polo mints – duly accepted. That was the end of hostilities. Three weeks later we were engaged and married exactly a year after that. Until the last war came we always had hot-pot for lunch on Christmas Eve and went to the theatre in the evening, with a large box of chocolates.

Mindful of what had happened about Pierre, I decided not to tell Mother about my engagement until she had had an opportunity to meet Randall, otherwise I knew that I should be ordered to return to England forthwith and told that no engagement could take place without parental approval. Randall went back to England in August 1925, a month before I did.

Mother like Randall personally but did not approve of his financial position which, admittedly at that time, did not look as healthy as it afterwards became. However, we were married in January 1926.

Mother died in June 1926. Father was a sick man by that time and continued to be so until he died in 1934.

Chapter 3

Some social changes since I was young

At this point of my narrative it is worthwhile, I think, to pause for a retrospective look at some of the social changes which have taken place between my young days and the present time.

Among the most important of these have been the lowering of class barriers, the more even spread of financial means and the lessening of poverty. The old idea of the 'working classes' as useful and necessary but inferior beings has at last disappeared. Naturally people continue to choose their friends mainly from those of more or less the same social and economic background but this is true at all levels. Public schools give an admirable education but attendance at one is no longer necessary to obtain an important job, far from it, the old school tie can sometimes be a disadvantage now. As to average incomes, surveys show, even allowing for the debasement of the currency which has taken place, how much better off a great majority of people are than 50 or 60 years ago. But I have no sympathy for those who wish to abolish all real wealth: to do so would make a negligible difference, spread over the whole population or dropped into the Treasury coffers, and it is the well-to-do who maintain a number of industries and enterprises with their yachts, costly cars, expensive clothes, jewellery and the like (which bring in large sums by way of VAT), without which many skills would be lost and more people unemployed. The greater the number of people the rich employ, the better. But the lessening of poverty, brought about to a considerable extent by taxation of the better-off is surely one of our better achievements.

I remember when I was young seeing in the streets dirty, tattered, often barefoot children who looked and were ill-nourished. Some were sickly and listless although others seemed tough enough and very active in spite of their skinniness and lack of clothing. For instance, little boys who chased after 'growlers' (horse-drawn four-wheel cabs) and clambered on to the rear axle for a ride and those who ran like greyhounds after snatching a bun or whatever from a shop or stall. Sometimes recently I have watched children coming out of a state school, taller, sturdier, obviously well-fed and almost invariably better-dressed than their forebears and felt very thankful.

I recall hearing about rather than seeing the ramshackle, cold, damp and verminous urban slums where slatternly women with squalling children and men, whose only solace was to get drunk when they could, eked out a wretched existence. There was a wide-spread belief that if you were taken into hospital you never came out alive and a common dread of ending one's days in a workhouse was felt by town-dwellers and country-dwellers alike.

The awakening of social conscience to the lot of the very poor is by no means a modern development. Those poor 'in very deed' were accepted as being a charge on public benevolence by the reign of Queen Elizabeth I. In 1572 an Act was passed instructing local authorities (mayors, sheriffs, bailiffs and others) to levy a reasonable rate on all local inhabitants and to settle the 'impotent poor' in 'permanent abiding places'. In 1958 'overseers' of the poor were appointed with the duty of seeing to the welfare of the poverty-stricken. I do not suppose that the poorhouses or workhouses were so unpopular then as they became before their abolition.

The Victorians who witnessed the Industrial Revolution

were not unmindful of those who did not benefit from it and numerous orphanages and similar institutions including the hospitals were built and maintained by voluntary contributions, a condition which lasted until the National Health Service legislation of 1946. The Church Army and the Salvation Army which do so much to help the needy still receive no State aid. Neither does a body of a different kind, the Royal National Lifeboat Institution whose men are so brave and efficient in rescuing those in peril on (and in) the sea, although nowadays they may be assisted by RAF helicopters or 'planes.

My grandfather was a keen supporter of a childrens' home. I remember that home from when I was about eight years old. One of the ways of raising money for it was to hold an annual childrens' ball there for the young of the well-to-do. We all came in our party clothes but before the fun began we were bidden to go upstairs and visit the inmates all tucked up in their little beds (with what seemed to me to be very ugly blankets). I remember wondering whether it would not make them envious to see us in all our finery about to have fun in which they could not join, but no, they loved it and looked forward to our visit as a great treat. (They did afterwards have all the jellies and trifles which were left over from our supper.) My visit started me wondering why we were so much more fortunate than they, but my questions to adults on the subject never received what seemed to me to be satisfactory answers. I cannot now recall what I was told but quite probably it was on the lines of the verse from a hymn:

> "The rich man in his castle,
> The poor man at his gate,
> God made them high or lowly
> And order'd their estate."

Incidentally this verse has disappeared from "All things bright and beautiful . . ." in the revised version of the Ancient and Modern hymn book. Good riddance!

In my young days, in village life there was generally a greater feeling of responsibility for one's neighbours than in towns, a feeling which I think persists to some extent to-day. And the Big House had an obligation (not invariably met I fear – some of the squirearchy were pretty mean) to visit and provide food for those who were sick. Further many landlords were prepared to wait for, or forego, the rent of a tenant who was ill. Perhaps this was a legacy from feudal times. But in many villages the Big House and its traditions have ceased to exist today.

It is gratifying to reflect that so much State aid today has not dried up the well of individual charity, as witness the millions given by rich and poor to succour famine victims in other parts of the world. And here at home the work of the National Health and Social Security authorities are supplemented by donations to the invaluable voluntary organisations for the handicapped, the blind, the deaf, the mentally ill, the old and the dying.

I would like to express my admiring tribute to those who give not only money to charitable causes but those who give time and sometimes their whole lives to helping other people. Starting at home, those who run the WRVS with its meals-on-wheels and other services; those who work for such organisations as The Samaritans, Alcoholics Anonymous and others. Perhaps most of all to those who leave home and go to work, often in appalling circumstances, in countries abroad, Africa and India for example. The world would be a poorer place without them. If I have one particular hero (which by statutory definition includes heroine) it is Mother Teresa. She is, I think, a perfect example of selfless, brave and practical Christian love. She enriches all our lives even though so few of us can go even a short way towards emulating her. She must cause great rejoicing in Heaven.

The decimation of our manhood in the 1914–18 war was of long-lasting effect. We lost so many men who should have been our leaders and reformers and enriched our national life. Our social and economic progress must have been considerably delayed by their loss. Almost the only good thing about that war, apart from the important fact that we avoided being conquered, seems to have been that, albeit temporarily, it ended the quite severe unemployment from which the country had been suffering at the end of the last and the beginning of this century. Perhaps I should add that women were given a new chance to show what they could do and that the treatment of wounds was improved when the medical profession had so many injured bodies on which to try out and find new methods.

The post-war boom in trade and industry lasted quite a while (as was the case after the 1939–45 war) but when this ended in the early 1930s the figures of unemployment soared. Those without employment received the dole but it was nothing like so adequate to their needs as unemployment pay and social security are today. Indeed, to a minority the adequacy of the present payments seems to be a disincentive to work. I am told that recently a local employment exchange had 400 job vacancies and was only able to fill 200 of them. And just the other day I spoke to a man whose employer was having difficulty in finding another car driver. I suggested that surely there must be plenty of available drivers on the local job list, but my informant disagreed and said that too many of them preferred unemployment pay and idleness to the grind of a daily job. No doubt such a minority exists but nobody will persuade me that the overwhelming majority of frustrated and aggrieved unemployed people would not accept any reasonable job which would give them back their self-respect and a decent wage.

To return to the slums to which I referred earlier, these have almost if not quite been replaced by better housing. There is of course a housing shortage today. It sometimes seems that trying to satisfy the demand for accommodation is rather like trying to stem the waves of the sea.

There are still landlords whose property is badly out of repair but they are gradually being made to mend their ways. The old excuse that the Rent Acts restrictions disabled them from keeping their property in order is losing its validity, particularly when improvement grants can be obtained. The worst conditions are usually to be found in multiple lettings in the same building.

A factor which has contributed to poor housing in recent times is that a number of the tower and other large blocks of council flats (all built with the best of intentions) were ill-designed to last for their intended span of years and have deteriorated rapidly. Repairing, replacing or even demolishing them at present day prices costs quite staggering sums of money. My own guess is that to do so satisfactorily would run into a good many billions. I fear that the task will have to be carried out piecemeal.

Of course there are still people who are slovenly by nature and more at home with dirt than with hygiene. I think that their numbers are fast decreasing, but perhaps a few of them will always be with us.

On the whole we can surely feel that, although society has not yet sufficiently improved the lot of its weaker brethren, we have gone a good way along the road. And this without revolution or violent measures. It would be possible for the nation to spend more on bettering conditions further but there comes a time when this process resembles eating the seed corn.

Women and children

Another of the important social changes which have taken place during my lifetime is the changing attitude to, and of, women. The suffragette movement at the beginning of the century is held by many people to have initiated the change. But I think that in fact it began in the last century. For example there were enough women doctors by May 1880 to found a federation of their own. Odd that they should have been considered sufficiently responsible to give medical treatment but not to vote and a number of men as well as women thought it unfair, but it is at least arguable that the activities of the suffragettes in chaining themselves to railings, throwing a brick through a politician's window and so on, delayed rather than speeded their enfranchisement. Such conduct shocked a good many people (including my parents) who took the view that if that was how some women behaved they were not fit to have the vote. It was surely the great contribution of women in the First World War which brought about, eg the Sex Disqualification (Removal) Act of 1919. Since then the process of what is called the 'emancipation' of women has accelerated, albeit many women today complain that they are still far from achieving equality. My own view is that complete equality is not practicable for the simple reason of the biological differences between the sexes. Women must still bear children unless we are to become manufactured robots. And maternal care of a young child is irreplaceable. Of course such care is not always practicable for economic reasons and is considered by other mothers to be incompatible with their pursuit of a career, which denies the child a lasting advantage. In another sphere a woman's physical strength and bodily hardness being less than a man's unfits her for certain activitiers. Exceptions to this proposition are to be found but it does not seem to me that, eg weight-lifting, boxing, rugby football or even soccer is a suitable sport for women. Other sports and pastimes abound in which they can compete with men, although in others such as championship tennis, ski-ing and swimming they cannot do so because of their different physiques. Similarly women are, in my view, unfit for some of the work done in heavy industry or, for that matter, in coal-mining. On the other hand I rejoice to see women holding important posts and making a splendid contribution, for example, to medicine and scientific research of all kinds. Nevertheless I believe that the joys and sorrows of bearing and rearing children, when this is possible, are better and more satisfying than the most brilliant career. If both can be combined, or succeed one another, that is fine but I wonder how many women who have satisfactorily fulfilled their maternal role to the detriment of their career really regret this. Perhaps it is nature's compensation for motherhood to men that they are usually able to satisfy their paternal instincts without damaging their careers!

On occasion Parliament in its anxiety to achieve sex equality has laid itself open to ridicule. The Sex Discrimination Act 1975 contained some gems:

Section 26 ". . . any establishment (a 'single-sex establishment') which admits pupils of one sex only or would be taken to admit pupils of one sex only if there were disregarded pupils of the opposite sex. . . ."

Section 38 forbade discriminatory advertisements and sub-s (3) laid it down that:

"use of a job description with a sexual connotation (such as waiter, salesgirl, postman or stewardess) shall be taken to indicate an intention to discriminate, unless the advertisement contains an indication to the contrary."

I cannot vouch for the accuracy of the story that after the Act was passed a firm which sold maternity gowns advertised in these terms:

"Wanted. Sales assistant of either sex. Must be pregnant."

The growth of scientific knowledge and its application to health care, means of communication and transport and broadcasting have certainly improved the amenities of life, if not always its quality.

Whatever may have been the advantages and disadvantages of the substitution of mechanical and electronic devices for the labours of men in factories, offices and almost everywhere else, there is one area where they are an unmitigated blessing. I refer to domestic appliances

The drudgery of the kitchen sink, the washtub and household cleaning have been splendidly lessened.

Incidentally we have gone so far in the sphere of electronics that the writers of science fiction must surely be finding it increasingly difficult to think of something which is not already fact, although I am told that an increasing number of serious-minded adults have taken to watching science fiction films as a guide to the future.

There is one aspect of research wizardry which causes me great unease: that is foetal research. Where does it stop? Artificial fertilisation of a wife's ovum with her husband's sperm in a test tube prior to insertion in the uterus is one thing and, when successful, has brought joy to a number of parents, but suppose that the insertion does not take place, how far should the resultant foetus be allowed to grow? Should it be grown in larger and larger test-tubes containing appropriate nutrients? I cannot see that, whatever the present position, this might not become a possibility. I would certainly forbid it by law.

There appears to me to be nothing wrong in artificial insemination when a husband's sperm is introduced (A.I.H.). But I have grave doubts about introduction of that of an unknown man (A.I.D.). I believe that some married couples accept this happily enough but it is easy to imagine unhappy situations which might arise from it, for example if a resultant child had highly undesirable characteristics which caused the couple great distress and which they might well attribute (rightly or wrongly) to inheritance from the unknown donor. They might then be sorry that the procedure ever took place. Obviously, naturally conceived children can and do sometimes exhibit such characteristics, but at least they are offspring with a blood relationship to both parents.

Artificial insemination of domestic animals appears to me to be entirely acceptable, just as is the production of hybrid plants, but animals and plants are not akin to human beings and entirely different considerations apply.

'Surrogate motherhood' is wholly undesirable in my opinion, not only because it involves an unnatural denial of the surrogate's maternal instincts, but also because it involves considerable risks. It is all very well to say that the whole process can be carried out in secrecy, but in all probability the secret will out. Not many women who are to receive the child can disappear for months on end, so relatives and friends must know that she has not been pregnant. What answer is to be given to their enquiries? The only way to deal with the situation seems to me to tell the child the truth as soon as he is old enough to take it in. This is also so, I think, in cases of adoption, but there the child's feelings towards both adoptive parents are involved, whereas he may react only against his supposed mother when he learns that he is not her son. The child who plays off one parent against the other is by no means an uncommon features of family life. Further the child of a surrogate mother is condemned to illegitimacy, whereas an adopted child is not. It is easy to say that illegitimacy is no longer the social disgrace that it used to be, but it still has serious legal disadvantages.

One of my strongest objections to maternal surrogacy is that almost inevitably it involves a woman using her body for commercial gain. This is what a prostitute does. It may be said that she has an altruistic as well as a commercial motive, but I have known of prostitutes who believed that they performed a valuable service to men. I would unhesitatingly support a ban on commercial surrogacy agencies.

It cannot fairly be said that I am lacking in sympathy for the unhappily childless, or that I fail to understand the basic and natural yearning for a child or the joy when the problem of childlessness is happily solved, but society has a duty to itself as well as to those who suffer and should not allow practices which are socially harmful in the long run.

A change for the worse

One of the saddest changes which I have witnessed is the lowering of the standard of behaviour in such large numbers of the population. Sexual morality is founded on good sense and what is best for society. The modern promiscuousness does not appear to me to have brought more happiness. Quite the contrary. The appalling number of broken homes and divorces has done enormous h arm to family life which is, or should be, the basis of the welfare of the community. Marital intercourse is, or ought to be, a source of joy and a bond between the spouses. I do not think that it is just the prating of an out-of-date old woman if I suggest that much of this may be spoiled if marriage is just one more in a series of sexual relationships. Who can be surprised if a son or daughter of a broken marriage says to himself or herself that his father or mother was unfaithful so why should he or she not be the same. On the other hand, to look on the brighter side, sometimes the child of a broken marriage may vow never to copy his parents. I have known a case where a very good-looking and attractive young woman, whose father's infidelity had caused much suffering, married a clergyman largely because it made her feel safe as he was unlikely to be unfaithful to her. Incidentally this turned out to be a very happy marriage with a number of happy children in a secure home. There must be a fair number of similar cases. It resembles the case of the child of a drunken father who becomes a teetotaller. I have known two or three instances of this happening and I would suppose that there are many more.

In conclusion

Life in modern times is certainly more comfortable and convenient than when I was young: it lasts longer with less illness owing to modern medical and surgical discoveries and inventions. But, with the exception of the very poor of my youth, I do not think that people generally are any happier today – rather the contrary.

Chapter 4

Married life

Leaving the wider issues about which I have been writing, I return to my personal story.

In a way Rushton's description of Randall, referred to in the second chapter, was accurate, but insofar as it gave the impression that he must be conceited and unapproachable it was wholly misleading. He was nothing of the sort: he was modest, kind, generous and sympathetic. He was also the most interesting and stimulating companion I have ever known. To the end of his life he was never boring to me or to anyone else and I was spared the fate of many wives who, however devoted to their husbands, sometimes have that glazed look of boredom in their eyes when they hear the same remarks or stories repeated over and over again. It was a source of great happiness to me that he regarded me as "the best wife any man ever had". This was much more than I deserved so I had all the more reason to be thankful that that was how he felt.

Let it not be thought after these panegyrics that we never fell out: of course we did. We were both fairly strong-willed and at times impatient. Certainly my temper was not always as well under control as it should have been. But as time passed we grew more alike in our ideas and tastes and in the end we often had the same thoughts without a word being spoken.

Manchester and a holiday

After we were married we lived first in Manchester. Randall was writing a thesis on classical influences in Shakespeare. On the strength of it he obtained his M.A. from Manchester University. Thereafter he became a lecturer in English literature. I had relatives and friends in Manchester, in particular there was a cousin of my mother's who was the wife of Arthur Lapworth, a professor of chemistry at the University there. They were childless and after my mother died liked to regard me as a daughter. Their unfailing kindness to Randall and myself was very pleasant for both of us.

During the early part of the marriage we were not well off financially, but most of the time we had a daily maid and contrived to have interesting holidays. In 1927 we had a burning desire to go to Italy for Easter, but one glance at the bank book revealed that this was wholly impracticable. Nothing daunted, Randall got himself appointed as courier and guide to a Workers' Educational Association tour of Italy, with a free place for me. This was the first time I had been in close contact with an assorted group of people of different backgrounds from my own though none of them came from what were then known as 'the working classes'. Apart from one member whom we dubbed 'the black widow' and who invariably complained, wanted something different and occasionally got lost, they were agreeable people, and all went well.

Some other holidays

Lindsay had a large Chrysler car and he, Randall and I went driving through Europe. Nothing unusual about that but what was unusual was our temerity in 1937 in driving down the middle of Yugoslavia as far as Dubrovnik. We met only one other car with G.B. plates. The

Shell company with commercial foresight had installed petrol pumps in a number of villages, but they were virtually unused then. More than once the man in charge, when you could find him, had no idea of how to operate the pump, neither could he read, so the instruction card was of no use to him. The local priest had to be sent for to read out the directions and supervise the operation.

The roads which we followed were sometimes no more than dirt tracks, some on the side of hills with barely enough width for the car and a nasty drop if you mismanaged things. You might be aware that there was a cart drawn by horses or oxen ahead of you because it created a cloud of dust, but it was impossible to overtake and you crept along behind it until you reached a better road.

Yugoslavia is a very different country today, of course, with a great many cars and good roads.

A nasty ending

In the summer of 1938 we all three went off again, this time taking in a bit of Poland and a good deal of Czecho-Slovakia. We ended up in Hungary on the shores of Lake Balaton in September. The only newspapers in any language we could read were at least four days old when they reached us and it suddenly struck us that war was probably imminent and that we were in entirely the wrong place. We left. That evening we reached Pilsen where the Skoda arms factories were. We met an Englishman who was in a position of some authority there and who enquired what on earth we were doing there, unless we wished to commit suicide. He was expecting the German bombers to attack that night. We went on to Marienbad. On the way there we heard shooting and the headlights revealed armed men half-hidden in the hedges. Marienbad was deserted, all the hotels were closed. We found a Sudeten German policeman who was uncomplimentary about our presence, but decided that we must find shelter and took us to an hotel. After much bell-ringing, banging and shouting the hotelier appeared. His protests were of no avail and we were admitted. The hotel was a large one and everything was covered with dustsheets which gave it a curiously eerie air, but beds were made up for us and we spent the night there. We debated whether to go on or to turn back and try to reach Italy or some other country where we could hope for a boat back to England, abandoning the car. In the end we decided to try to get across, and out of, Germany before the hostilities commenced. We started early in the morning. We bought something to eat and drink in the car so that we need not stop for meals.

At the German frontier we produced the usual collection of documents, carnet and so forth. We gathered that something was missing but we were all afflicted with an inability to understand German that day and finally we were allowed to proceed. We discovered afterwards that what we should have had was a military permit to be on the roads. We were not far into Germany before we met the German army in force moving east towards Czecho-Slovakia. There were men, guns, tanks and other vehicles. We were not popular; an armoured car tried to force us into the ditch and nearly succeeded; as we passed by it a machine gun was swung round on us and the rat-a-tat made a very unpleasant noise. I was sitting in the back of the car and comforted myself with the thought that machine gun bullets would not penetrate through the suitcases which were packed solid in the boot. In fact the gun must have been firing blanks because there was no mark on the car afterwards and no gunner could have missed at that range.

We approached the frontier post with a horrible feeling that we might not be allowed out of Germany. Officials came to the car to inspect passports and papers and I never saw a more welcome sight than the barrier as it lifted to let us out. Likewise the Belgian barrier lifted to let us in. We jumped out of the car, went into the guard post and demanded to see a senior army officer. It was about three o'clock in the morning by then but eventually an army captain arrived. We told him that we assumed that Britain and Belgium would again be allies in war and that we could give details of all the army dispositions we had seen from one side of Germany to the other if he would promise to telephone the information to the British War Office immediately. He said that he would and took lengthy notes of what we said.

Thereafter, at a more leisurely pace, we went further into Belgium and there we learned that while we were haring through Germany Mr Chamberlain had flown to Munich and averted immediate war. It was of course a relief in a way, but at the same time a bit of a sell. And although many of us were not taken in by the words "peace in our time" at least we had a year in which to start remedying the arms situation brought about by misguided pacifism.

Landing in Egypt

The last holiday which I will mention in detail was in 1960. We were in Jordan and the Lebanon and flew to Cairo. The plane from Beirut was overladen and could not gain sufficient height, so we had to return to Beirut while some freight was off-loaded. Finally, away we went and over the red desolation of the Sinai desert (which aroused my sympathy for the Israelites who had to cross it as they fled from Pharaoh). That most unpleasant wind, the Hamcin, was blowing, making it a very bumpy flight. We reached Cairo airport and had almost touched down when some lunatic drove a jeep across the runway. We hit it with our undercarriage. We saw the jeep flying through the air and disappearing into space. (We heard afterwards that the driver was thrown clear and survived.) But our undercarriage was a buckled mass of twisted metal (again, as we learned afterwards) and it was a considerable feat on the part of the Arab pilot to get up into the air again. We then had to burn up fuel before crash-landing. Round and round we flew while we could see below us the fire-engines and ambulances collecting for our arrival. I dare say that it was really no more than half-an-hour before we came down on the soft sand at the end of the runway. The plane tipped over on to its nose, then fell back as fire swept along the outside of the cabin and was almost immediately extinguished by the sandstorm the landing had created. Passengers were told to open the rear door of the plane and jump out on to the sand. As we sprang out of our seats, from sheer force of habit, Randall snatched his hat from the overhead rack. When we were a safe distance away from the plane he looked at the hat and said disgustedly "This isn't my hat". A moment later an American couple with whom we had made friends in Jerusalem emerged from the plane and joined us. The husband said crossly "I've left my hat on the plane". At which Randall (without batting an eyelid) said "It's alright, I've brought it out for you". The American was full of gratitude. We never disillusioned him although he and his wife have remained good friends ever since. If they should read this, they will know the awful truth at last. (Odd how much importance some men attach to their hats!)

The plane was an ancient Dakota and its strong underbelly does not have its like today. Nobody suffered anything worse than bruises. If one must crash, I do recommend Cairo with its runways ending in soft sand.

Randall and I were due to dine at the British Embassy that evening. There was a sympathetic telephone message to the effect that although a number of people wished to meet us, everyone would understand if we did not wish to go after our ordeal. Not go indeed! The experience had filled us with an enormous zest for life and we both disgraced ourselves by accepting second helpings at dinner.

There were many more holidays, usually to Italy, but sometimes to the United States and Canada and Africa.

Leicester

In 1930 we left Manchester and went to live in Leicester, where Randall lectured in the Adult Education Department of the University College (now Leicester University). He was very interested in this kind of teaching: he felt that too many adults who left school at 14, and many who had longer education, were missing so much of what literature can offer. Certainly he received much gratitude for his work. The Principal of the College was Professor Attenborough, father of Richard and David who were delightful little boys. They early showed a spirit of enterprise: when they were about nine and six years old respectively, they persuaded their parents to let them have the use of a large room in the house in order to present a play, with no adult assistance or interference. The parents assumed that the audience would consist of the boys' own friends and perhaps a few parents beside themselves. When it was almost time for the performance to begin, Mrs Attenborough was horrified to see the Mayoral car draw up and disgorge the Lord Mayor and Lady Mayoress, complete with chains of office. The boys had issued the invitation to them and other local bigwigs who did not suspect that the invitation was given other than with parental knowledge and approval. I believe the performance was a great success.

When we had a larger home, it occurred to us that children's games had been immense fun and that it was a pity that one no longer played them once one grew up. So we had 'children's parties for grown-ups'. Nobody over 35 was invited and guests were asked to wear old clothes. We played, for example, Musical Chairs, Blind-Man's Bluff, Nuts-In-May, Two's-and-Three's, Balloon Tennis, Hide-and-Seek-in-the-Dark and had

45

Treasure Hunts. When exhaustion set in we consumed colossal piles of sandwiches and drank coffee. Perhaps 20 or 30 people were invited at a time and I cannot remember ever having a refusal. I fear that young adults today, even if they knew how to play some of the games, would think this form of entertainment ridiculous, but we all enjoyed it very much indeed.

More about the marriage of Randall and myself will inevitably appear from later chapters.

Chapter 5

John

This will be a very short chapter. It would be impossible to omit any reference to our son, John, but to write about him at length would be too painful. He was born in August 1928 in Manchester. No parents could have been happier at his arrival than Randall and I were. We had agreed that we wanted to have four children. When he was about 18 months old he had what was then thought to be an infantile convulsion. In fact it was the inception of epilepsy. Years later the doctors advanced the theory that he had had non-infectious meningitis, which would have given the appearance of nothing more than a severe cold. He had had such a cold some time before the first seizure but seemingly had recovered from it, albeit slowly. As a result of the meningitis scarring, the circulation of the cerebro-spinal fluid was inhibited, causing increasing brain damage. He died when he was fourteen and a half years old. Reluctantly we agreed to an autopsy because we were persuaded that this might help the doctors in the treatment of other afflicted children. The findings confirmed the diagnosis.

He had been a very happy baby and was a very jolly little boy, full of fun, physically active and able to run surprisingly fast. He very early manifested a love of music, not only for simple tunes but also for classical music, but he made little progress mentally as the years went by. Naturally this was a devastating sorrow to Randall and myself and by the time John was seven years old the strain of looking after him and trying to teach him to do simple things was seriously affecting my health. We were strongly advised that it would be better for him to be in professional hands and with other children in need of special care and training and so he went to a Rudolf Steiner Home. He did make somewhat better progress there at first and I can never be thankful enough for the skilled and devoted care he received, but after the initial improvement, his condition gradually deteriorated, as was apparent every time we visited him. In February 1943 he caught influenza which turned to pneumonia and he died.

Chapter 6

Going to the Bar, with interruptions

Randall's interest in literature and adult education were by no means exclusive; he was also interested in art, philosophy and most particularly in law. For years he had wished that he had become a barrister. In 1936 he decided that it was not too late at 38 years of age to read for the Bar. I used to 'hear' him on the subjects he was studying. I became greatly interested in them myself and after a year or so he said that I knew the subjects better than he did and that I too ought to go to the Bar. My first response was that the idea was ridiculous. I was then 32 years old and for the 14 years since I had left school I had lived a domestic and social life and done nothing else. I was enthralled by Randall's idea, which had never entered my head until he spoke of it, but I was convinced that I should never pass the Bar examinations and that even if, by some miracle, I should do so, I should certainly not be any good as a barrister. Randall disagreed. After much discussion we decided that I should consult cousin Arthur Lapworth, whose professorial experience should have made him a good judge of students or would-be students. We agreed that we would be bound by his view. So I asked him if he thought that I could possibly pass the Bar exams. I remember his answer: "On your head". That was it.

Studying and dining

In November 1937 I joined Randall as a student member

of the Inner Temple. We studied together, which made it easier for both of us. Randall continued his lecturing and we went together to 'keep terms' at the Inner Temple, that is to say that we dined in hall the requisite number of times in each term. People are apt to think this is a curious custom, but it has its origins, like so much else in the law, in sound practical considerations. Centuries ago, when the Inns of Court were first turning students into barristers, there were few, if any, law reports and there was a dearth of textbooks. How then were the students to learn the law? One method devised was for barristers and students to dine together – three students to one barrister. During dinner the barrister held forth on legal topics and answered questions. This somewhat dyspeptic practice has long since ceased, but compulsory dining continues. A further and lasting advantage was, and is, that compulsory attendance at the Inn of Court helps to foster a desirable collegiate spirit. Today this spirit is also encouraged in many other ways.

The first of the Part I exams was Roman law. This one could take without knowing any Latin, but it was easier if one had some knowledge of that very dead language. Randall's knowledge of it was very much better than my schooldays' recollection but, most unfairly, he obtained a pass and I got a first – my only one in all the Bar exams. He was delighted; it showed how right he had been in his insistence that I should become a barrister. I confess that sometimes while the process continued I had to force myself back to the books instead of playing tennis or badminton or otherwise amusing myself and that sometimes I yielded to temptation. We worked without tuition until it came to reading for the finals. Then we spent about three months at Gibson & Weldons' cramming course in London. We lived in the Temple while doing so.

Wartime – Bar finals

The final examinations were to be held at the beginning of October 1939. When war was declared on 3 September of that year I remember vividly the almost over-whelming horror it inspired and yet the relief one felt that this country had stopped its cowardly appeasement and would at last stand up to the monster that was Hitler, instead of letting him dictate to us. Even before the declaration everyone was expecting it. Bar students were informed that in the event of war the Bar finals examinations would not be held. At about the same time a cousin of mine who worked at St George's Hospital telephoned to enquire what I was doing and when I answered "Nothing", she asked me to go the the Medical School canteen at the Hospital which had been run, I think, by a woman and her daughters, all of whom had departed precipitately for the country to escape the anticipated bombing of London, leaving the canteen unattended and useless for several days. Students had ceased to use the canteen but the doctors depended upon it as a source of food and drink in the hospital.

My task was to provide breakfasts, lunches, teas, dinners and drinks for medical staff whose numbers could only be roughly estimated. I knew nothing about catering for perhaps a dozen or more people. Fortunately the butcher did know and I could guess about everything else. I coped alone for the first few days, then one other volunteer arrived and later still so did another, a charming woman who brought her butler with her. His demeanour on arrival was of the impeccable dignity of his calling, but it was not long before he too was doing everything at the double. He was a great help with the 'hole-in-the-wall' through which beer was sold to the hospital workmen. The necessary hours of work were from about 8.00 am to 9.00 pm. One night when I returned to the Temple and faced the 81 stone stairs up to the flat, I realised that my feet would go no further so I went up on my hands and knees. The workload increased when we were required to provide breakfast every morning for a number of special constables who had been on night duty in the Hyde Park Corner area. Their appetites were prodigious. Happily, before the end of the month a professional caterer was employed to run the canteen and at about the same time the Bar students were informed that the finals examinations would be held after all. So I was able to leave the canteen with a good conscience and return to my books. It was curious how much I had managed to forget in so short a time. Any dreams I may have entertained about getting a first were dashed. In fact no firsts were awarded then, but I came second in the second class, which, all things considered, was exceedingly fortunate. Poor Randall, who had not had the requisite time for preparation, failed and had to take the exams again. But he was delighted that if one of us had to fail, it should not be me. It was a splendid "I told you so" situation and plainly if it had not been for his insistence and encouragement I should never have started.

Because I had got through the exams in a shorter time than that allotted, I could not be called to the Bar until the summer of 1940. Our occupation of the Temple flat had ended in October 1939 and we had returned then to Leicester. There Randall became a pupil in local Bar Chambers until 1940 when he joined the staff of the British Council and was appointed Council representative in Milan.

Back to Manchester

I packed up, stored the furniture and departed for Manchester where I went to live with Mrs Lavinia Rée, the mother of some friends of mine. She had three sons and five daughters but the sons were in the forces and the daughters were married, leaving her alone in the large family house, except for two maids. The youngest son,

Harry, as is well known, did very brave work when he was parachuted into France and worked with the French Resistance Movement. The arrangement worked very well for both of us and we became very fond of each other. She was American by birth and was one of the most admirable characters I have ever known. No doubt she would have been startled at such an idea but I am not alone in thinking that she was very near to sainthood.

It was for me to find war-work to do: I answered an advertisement and joined the Ministry of Information Censorship Division which was housed in a large, requisitioned department store in Manchester. Applicants were interviewed, given a short course of instruction and thereafter took a written examination. After the Bar exams that was 'kids'-stuff' for me. It was a dreary job but it seemed to be a necessary one. The salary of £3 a week was the first money I had ever earned (except for being paid by members of the family and their friends for embroidery work and also having had one article published in the 'Nursery World' magazine many years before). At one stage I worked with three somewhat disgruntled servicemen: a naval commander with a duodenal ulcer which kept him from going to sea, an army major considered by the authorities (but not himself) to be too old for active service and an R.A.F. officer who was too fat to fly. I was not at all suitable as a civil servant. The hierarchy and the red tape irked me and I was more than once hauled up for exceeding my powers when trying to get things done. I was in the happy position of not minding if I was sacked and rather enjoyed stirring up the establishment which, anyway, did not seem to like being lumbered with temporaries.

Randall was not in Italy for very long. In June 1940 Count Ciano, Mussolini's son-in-law who was Foreign Minister and whom Randall knew, telephoned to tell him to get out of Italy fast. Randall had of course known that Italy would be coming into the war against us very soon and had sent off most of his possessions to the

British Embassy in Paris. He took a train, I think to Como, and then walked over the hills into Switzerland. At Chiasso he found a train going to Monte Carlo where he stayed overnight in an hotel where the only other guests were Hugo Thyssen, the German arms manufacturer, who had apparently incurred Hitler's displeasure, and a member of a well-known English literary family who had earlier been lecturing for the British Council in Italy and who expressed his belief that if the Germans invaded France they would nevertheless respect the independence of Monaco – a view which Randall did not share. In Monte Carlo Randall found that he could still get to Paris by train and arrived there as the German army approached. He left by the last plane for England carrying Embassy personnel. Flying over the Channel they saw what was to both passengers and crew the then incomprehensible sight of lines of unrecognisable craft travelling between Dunkirk and England.

Randall came to see me briefly in Manchester, before returning to work for the British Council in London, living in an hotel. Christmas came and as he had leave he joined me in Manchester. I had told him that he would be able to sleep better as nothing much in the way of air raids happened there. On the night of his arrival, the Manchester blitz took place.

London and pupillage

I had already applied for a transfer to London but was told that transfers were not granted to temporary civil servants, so I sent in my resignation and joined Randall as soon as it expired in January 1941. Thereafter I was informed that I could, after all, be transferred, but before that could take place, by chance, I met Paul Sandlands, K.C., a Bencher of the Inner Temple, who had sponsored my entry as a student and proposed my call to the Bar. He asked what I was doing and whether anyone who was not a barrister could do the job. My answer to the latter question was, of course, "yes". Then he said that if I wanted to be of real use in the war effort, I should start at the Bar and do what he called "the dirty work", that is Poor Prisoners' Defences, Service divorces and many other small and illpaid cases which were in danger of being neglected because so many of the young barristers who would normally have taken them were away on war service and the more senior barristers were overworked and unable to cope with everything. I had earlier intended not to start at the Bar while so many of the young men were away, because to do so would be to gain an unfair advantage over them. But Paul Sandlands was very persuasive and after time for reflection and discussion with Randall I decided that my conscience would be clear if I did what I was longing to do. In January 1941 Paul Sandlands arranged for me to become a pupil of a member of his Chambers, Geoffrey Howard, who afterwards became a county court judge. I was told very firmly that at the end of my pupillage I should not be able to remain in those Chambers but that a seat would be found for me in other Chambers. This was because the senior clerk, apart from anyone else, would not wish to have a woman member of Chambers. Women at the Bar were not generally regarded as a good financial proposition in those days. However, before my pupillage ended to my great joy I was invited to stay on and very happily remained a member of the same Chambers for as long as I was at the Bar.

Chapter 7

At the junior Bar

Geoffrey Howard was an admirable pupil-master. He was a literary man as well as a lawyer and had been a friend of G. B. Shaw, G. K. Chesterton, Hilaire Belloc and other well-known authors of his day. He had written novels and verses under the name of Marmaduke Dixey. His written Bar pleadings were said to be the best in the Temple and were excellent models to try to emulate. A pupil sees all his master's papers, is present at his conferences and goes with him to court. As one progresses in one's pupillage one tries one's hand at drafting the master's pleadings. To begin with these are usually scrapped or mercilessly amended by the master, but the proud day may come when he says, "I'll sign that as it is". Without such training one is not fit to be a practising member of the Bar, which is why it has been made obligatory.

First briefs

As I had been called to the Bar by the time I became a pupil, I was theoretically qualified already to take any briefs which came my way. It was not too long before the first one did. It was a matrimonial case in a magistrates' court (then referred to as a police court). I took advice as to how to conduct it, but have virtually no recollection of it, save that it was all over in a few minutes, much to

56

my relief. The next was a Rent Act case in a county court, in which a landlord was seeking possession of his house from the tenant on the ground of nuisance. I was appearing for the tenant who was a police officer and to whom losing the case would have been a serious matter, apart from being made homeless. To say that I was terrified out of my wits is no exaggeration. When the case ended I came out of court with the symptoms of shock. My face was chalk-white and I could remember nothing at all of what had taken place in court except for two matters: we had won and kind Judge Earengey had said during his judgment, "Mrs Lane very wisely refrained from pursuing that line of cross-examination". I was conscience-stricken at receiving the compliment because it had not occurred to me that such a line of cross-examination could be pursued: if it had, I should probably have pursued it.

Criticisms are sometimes made of the robes worn in court by judges and barristers. There are powerful and, to my mind, convincing reasons for retaining them which I will not canvas here, but I will add one of my own which is that it is an immense comfort to a nervous young practitioner to know that, however green and incompetent he may feel, at least he looks like a barrister.

I interpolate here that under the Interpretation Acts 'masculine' includes 'feminine'. So when I write 'he' this includes 'she', which saves the wearisome repetition of 'he or she', or the use of 'person' when 'man' would do just as well.

Joining a circuit

Perhaps I was fortunate in doing few cases in magistrates' courts and having my early work mainly in London county courts. After I became a pupil I joined the Midland Circuit (now the Midland and Oxford Circuit) and "showed my face", as the senior clerk so inelegantly put it, at the Quarter Sessions and Assizes on the Circuit. This meant attending the sittings without any briefs and just hoping for a dock brief, a Poor Prisoner's Defence, or a last-minute returned brief. It was encouraging that one such quite often came my way, even if this was only because during the war there were so few juniors available for the purpose. There were disappointments of course, in particular I recall being present at a conference with Geoffrey Howard and one of his solicitor clients. At the end of the conference the solicitor said to me, "Can I have a word with you outside?" We repaired to the corridor with my hopes soaring, I was sure that he was going to say that he had a brief for me. He first asked me if I would do him a favour (from which I assumed that the brief would carry only a minimal fee) but what he went on to say was, "Will you make sure that Mr Howard gets to Court on Monday by 10.30?" Dear Geoffrey, he had many accomplishments but punctuality was not always his strong suit. Later on, the same solicitor did send me a few of his lesser briefs.

My first criminal case was a Poor Prisoner's Defence at Bedfordshire Quarter Sessions. I was asked by the Court to defend a man who was unrepresented. As usual, prosecuting counsel lent me his copy of the depositions (ie the evidence recorded in the committal proceedings before magistrates). The prosecuting counsel was T. R. Fitzwalter Butler, a stern but always fair prosecutor (one-time editor of *Archbold*, for many years the standard criminal textbook) and always a good friend to junior barristers in need of advice – as I certainly was. I asked him whether there seemed to be any defence to the charge of stealing from an employer. His answer was that none was apparent from the depositions. When I read them I could only agree with his view. Then I saw my client in the cells. He did not seem to me to be able to offer any defence but said firmly that he would plead not guilty and give evidence on his own behalf. If I had been a little more experienced I should have advised him to plead guilty which, as it turned out, would have been bad advice. The case looked no better at the conclusion of the evidence and the summing-up was necessarily unfavourable to the defence. When the jury retired to consider their verdict it seemed inevitable that they would find the man guilty. No so! To everyone's astonishment, including my own, he was acquitted. The Chairman was so amazed that he gave an audible "Good God!" I am not being modest when I say that the probable explanation was that the jury had recognised how inexperienced defending counsel was and had thought that there must have been a defence of some kind which had not been put before them.

I recall my first case of a sexual offence. I had of course read and learned about sexual offences from *Archbold* and the relevant statutes, but there was a great deal of difference between the cold print and instructions to defend a man on charge of indecent assault on a young girl. I was so horrified and disgusted with the details that I burst into tears, threw the papers into the waste paper basket, muttering to myself that I would *not* take part in such a filthy case. After a while I pulled myself together, retrieved the papers and studied and made notes on them. When it came to the trial I was wholly unperturbed. There is something about the clinical and impersonal atmosphere of a court which nullifies any prudish or squeamish reaction to the facts of the case; they become provable or disprovable like the facts of any other case. I never again boggled at cases of sexual offences.

In those days a dock brief carried the magnificent fee of one guinea and £1 3s 6d had to be extracted from the defendant before counsel could act for him. The half-crown was the barrister's clerk's entitlement. Usually a prison officer had the money ready out of what the man had when he was received into prison or surrendered to his bail. A dock brief entitled the defendant to choose any barrister in court in robes (except the prosecutor) to defend him. It was a boon to beginners but after one had acquired a practice it could be a menace because it was

59

At the junior Bar

obligatory to take the case and if it lasted over the day this might mean returning another and more lucrative case starting the next day. Sometimes one heard a whisper that a dock brief application was going to be made and one could nip out of court so as to avoid being caught in that situation. The single fee was all one received even if the case lasted for days.

Poor Prisoners' Defences paid three guineas. Poor Persons' Divorces which were undefended paid one guinea, except those of armed services personnel which earned no fee. All these arrangements for representation have now been superseded by legal aid.

Looking back at the fee book for my first year at the Bar, the fees were one or two guineas, less frequently three or five. There was one splendid fee of 50 guineas when I had a leader and was automatically entitled to an amount equal to two-thirds of his fee. All this added up to 160 guineas, which more than paid my six-months' pupillage fee, Chamber and Circuit expenses and was considered to be a remarkable achievement. Usually at that period one had to be more, sometimes considerably more, than a year at the Bar to make one's expenses. Young barristers today would laugh at such earnings. But of course their expenses are much higher and they would no doubt be envious of my contribution of a mere £60 a year for rent and other Chambers expenses, and of Circuit hotel bills of about £1 or so, dinner included.

Attributes for success

What are the attributes which make for success at the Bar? Different people would give different answers to that question but, without attempting a comprehensive enumeration (which would be virtually impossible) I suggest that among the most important attributes are, first, good health and stamina. It can be very hard to battle against, and perhaps try to conceal, ill-health and I have known few successful barristers who have achieved this. Then comes a capacity for hard work and concentrated application to the matter in hand. Next I put good temper, or at any rate, the ability to control and conceal any natural ill-temper. Counsel who loses his temper in court usually fails, at least temporarily, to conduct the case to the best of his ability. Indeed, control of all one's emotions and facial expressions is important. A compliment once paid to me by another barrister which gave me particular pleasure was to the effect that if I got a really bad answer from a witness my expression never changed and I went on as if nothing had gone wrong. Perhaps a little obvious satisfaction at a particularly good answer may sometimes be permissible, but usually one does better to proceed without letting a witness see what one is thinking or feeling. One should be intellectually but not emotionally involved in one's case. Objectivity should be preserved. I would also refer to the voice of a barrister. If a judge or jury has to listen to counsel over a long period it helps if he has a pleasing voice, or at any rate one which is not harsh or grating. Of course I do not mean that a barrister must have an 'Oxford accent'. I have known a number of barristers with a distinctly local accent who were a pleasure to hear. I believe that there was a High Court judge in the not-too-distant past who was short of his H's. A very high voice in a woman barrister can be a real disadvantage, particularly if, as in one or two instances I have known, it tends to get higher and higher as the case proceeds. When I endeavoured to sing it was as a contralto which was fortunate for me. Also, although I had not realised it until I was told so by George Pleydell-Bancroft (then the Clerk of the Assize of the Midland Circuit and a member of the well-known theatrical family) it seems that I had the ability to pitch and modulate my voice to the acoustics of the particular court in which I was appearing. Whether this was due to my having had singing and elocution lessons I do not know, this may have helped, although there are many barristers who do so instinctively and who have never

61

had a singing or elocution lesson in their life. This is a very useful attribute and a barrister who shouts or one who is inaudible is not beloved of the judges.

Last but not least as an aid to success I would list good luck. One needs good luck at the Bar, particularly in the early stages. I think that I was lucky: I remember one instance when I certainly was. I received a returned brief in the Court of Appeal for the next day: it was an appeal against a judgment in favour of a boy who had been injured by a thresher or some other piece of farm machinery. This was in May 1943 and was my first appearance in the Court of Appeal except for once in 1942 when I put in a nominal appearance behind a leader in place of the real junior and had nothing to say or do. In the 1943 case one of the obstacles in the path of the respondent farmer, for whom I was appearing, was that the judgment had been given by the late Mr Justice Croom-Johnson (father of the present High Court judge of that name⋆) who had a reputation for wide knowledge of the law and accuracy in its application. I was in difficulty because of the inadequacy of the time I had had to study the relevant authorities. I was addressing that Court when one of their Lordships asked me a question (a disconcerting though sometimes helpful habit which judges have). I had no idea what the right answer should be and in my nervousness was flicking over the pages of one of the authorities when suddenly my eye was caught by the very passage which contained an answer to the question. (If I had had more time to prepare the case I ought to have known that it was there.) If that was not a piece of luck I do not know what it was. The fact that the appeal failed, as it was almost bound to do, did not detract from my thankfulness for having been saved at an awkward moment. The name of the case was *Holdman v Hamlyn* and it was reported in the Law Reports, the first case of mine which attained that distinction. This did me no harm at all.

⋆Now Lord Justice Croom-Johnson

Women at the Bar

In my early days at the Bar there were few women practising and even fewer with a good practice. There was still a certain amount of prejudice against women barristers, although the first of them had been called to the Bar as long ago as 1922. It was after the Sex Disqualification (Removal) Act of 1919 was passed that they were admitted as students of the Inns of Court and could be called to the Bar after passing the examinations. Gray's Inn had the distinction of being one of the first of the Inns of Court to call women to the Bar. As part of the Call ceremony the Treasurer of the Inn makes a speech of welcome to the Barristers who have just been called. But on the occasion to which I refer the then Treasurer of Gray's Inn (long since dead) was not in sober mood and so far forgot himself as to say that women were quite unfitted for the Bar and added "The only time when the male intellect descends to that of the female is when the male is drunk." At which a voice from the back of the hall was heard to say "I see. Down to the she in sips" – a nice quip but I like to think that the Treasurer would have been surprised (not to say flabbergasted) to learn the facts that in the year 1984 of the 5,203 practising Barristers 641 would be women, that of the 545 practising Queen's Counsel 11 would be women and that there would be 15 Circuit judges and three High Court judges who were women.

I think that the early prejudice against women barristers was mainly on the part of the litigants rather than of solicitors. No solicitor was ever tactless enough to tell me that he had had difficulty in persuading a client to agree to a woman being briefed on his behalf but I have no doubt that this happened on occasions. Indeed, I know it did once when, after rather a good win in a difficult case, I received a somewhat left-handed compliment from the lay client who ended by saying, ". . . and I take back everything I said to the solicitor about having a woman barrister." On another occasion the opposite occurred when, as the solicitor told me, a man walked into his office and said, "Good morning – My name is so-and-so. I am charged with embezzlement. Can you get Mrs Lane to defend me? If not I am going elsewhere."

Sometimes of course the prejudice was on the part of solicitors. After one of my early cases in the county court, in which judgment was given for my client, my clerk asked the instructing solicitor on the other side how he liked "being beaten by a woman". The answer was something kind about my conduct of the case but an emphatic statement that in no circumstances would his firm ever brief a woman. He was a member of one of London's most respected firms of solicitors. Wild horses would not drag the name from me – they could not because I have forgotten which firm it was. I feel sure that the firm has changed its views by now.

It has not been unknown for the lay client himself, at any rate in criminal cases to make his opinion of his counsel known publicly. Years ago now, one dissatisfied prisoner in open court called his woman counsel "a cauliflower-headed bitch." Come to think of it, the top of a bar wig does bear a certain resemblance to a cauliflower, but no doubt the inaccuracy of the rest of the description was dealt with by the judge. On the other hand I have heard a prisoner in the dock just after the jury retired to consider their verdict say to his woman barrister "Win or lose, thank you very much for everything you have done for me." And I suppose that many counsel of both sexes who have defended in a criminal case have been warmly thanked for their efforts privately.

When I first went on circuit the practical arrangements for women barristers were non-existent. At Assize Courts and Quarter Sessions Courts there was a men's robing-room, which I was expected to share. I did not endear myself to those in charge of the court buildings by agitating for separate accommodation. But in the end I succeeded except in one Quarter Sessions Court in

Lincolnshire where lack of room made it impossible: there was just one large room in which counsel robed, solicitors left their hats and coats and police officers deposited their helmets. Very matey, but undignified.

There was also difficulty about a separate robing-room in some of the county courts in and around London. In one of them my persistence was rewarded by the exclusive use of a room on the door of which was a large notice 'GAS KEEP OUT'.

Among male members of the Bar I met with no sign of resentment or any obvious feeling of masculine superiority. On the contrary, they were uniformly kind and as helpful to me as, traditionally, they are towards one another. A barrister in difficulty over some legal point can always go to another with greater or more specialised knowledge to ask for advice and, no matter how busy the latter may be, this is always forthcoming. Bearing in mind what one or two other women barristers have told me of their experiences, I think that I was very fortunate, lucky perhaps, in this regard.

As to the judges' attitude to a woman barrister almost without exception they were kind. The last thing one wanted was extra kindness because one was a woman but I did not feel that I received more than the usual consideration judges try to show to all beginners. Once I had become an established practitioner I think that I was treated in the same way as any other member of the Bar. There were two exceptions, two judges who made it painfully obvious that a woman's appearance before them was unwelcome. They are both dead now: there is no need to mention their names. There were judges who were more difficult to get on with than others, but male barristers also found them so.

Judicious approach

There is considerable scope for a barrister to adapt his

presentation of a case to suit a particular judge. One could say things to one judge which one would not dare to say to another. As an illustration of this let me refer to a wartime case in which, to the best of my recollection the facts were that a private in the Polish army based in this country believed that a senior officer was making advances to the private's wife. The officer was in the habit of riding a bicycle back to his quarters each evening. The private lay in wait for him in a wood through which he would pass. By chance, in the wood the private saw a woodman's broom with a long, strong handle. He used it to attack the officer and inflicted severe injuries which might have proved fatal to a man with a thinner skull. At the trial before the late Mr Justice Cassels the prosecution dropped the charge of attempted murder and accepted a plea of guilty to unlawful wounding with intent to do grievous bodily harm. It was of course a serious offence but prosecuting counsel managed to create an atmosphere of portentous gloom. As the Judge listened he looked increasingly grave. I was appearing for the private with the task of trying to mitigate the sentence which I felt was growing longer and longer in the Judge's mind. I wondered what on earth I could do to lighten the atmosphere so, trying to look cheerful but with great inner trepidation, when I rose to address the Judge I began by saying, "As your Lordship appreciates, this is the case of a Pole who hit a Pole with a pole." It took the Judge so much by surprise that he had to suppress a laugh. Thereafter I was the better able to urge in his favour the previous efforts of the private to end the suspected association peacefully and the great provocation it had been to him. The sentence was surprisingly short. I think that Mr Justice Cassels was perhaps the only judge before whom I should have had the temerity to start as I did. Many judges would sternly have rebuked me for unseemly levity, which would have done my client no good at all.

As the war years passed life became increasingly

difficult. Circuit travel was no joke at all. Petrol was severely rationed, trains were few and often very late, restaurant cars disappeared and hotel accommodation was scarce or sometimes unobtainable. But one had to be at court on time. I was only late twice: once on the way to Grimsby County Court when the train stuck in a snowdrift and once at Birmingham Assizes. On the latter occasion another barrister and I were asked by the late Mr Justice Lewis to undertake the defence of two men in the dock before him. Neither of us had expected to be appearing in Birmingham on the following day. We tried telephoning almost every hotel in the town without being able to get rooms. We asked the police if they could help and we even suggested police cells but they, like the hotel rooms, were full up. So there was nothing for it but to go back to London and return by a very early train the next morning. All should have been well except that a bomb had been dropped on the railway line which made us an hour or more late at court. Mr Justice Lewis could be very fierce if he was annoyed and although we had such a cast-iron excuse we were dithering with apprehension. But when he heard our heart-rendering tale he was sympathetic and charming about it so all was well.

Perhaps today lateness at court is not regarded as so heinous an offence as it used to be, but when I became a judge any barrister who appeared late before me could expect a severe wigging unless he had a really good excuse. Little nonsenses like unexpectedly heavy traffic or a narrowly missed train got nowhere with me. Barristers are not the only ones who can be late: one of our elderly and somewhat irascible judges was trying a jury case at Lincoln when a woman juror arrived back at court after the mid-day adjournment 20 minutes late and bearing a laden shopping basket. The Judge delivered a withering reprimand but the juror was unwithered and retorted, "Young man if you had seven mouths to feed you would be late back from shopping." Not a further word came from the Judge and everyone in court breathed again.

With hindsight I regret that I did not preserve any of my dozens of Bar notebooks, so I am largely dependent on my memory in trying to recall cases in which I was concerned. I have my diaries but these contain no more than the names of cases which I can find anyway in the fee-books kept by my clerk, which I have retained. I have derived a little assistance from newspaper cuttings which I kept with decreasing regularity for the first three years or so in practice. Additionally I have a large number of letters which I wrote to an old cousin (Mrs Lapworth, referred to in an earlier chapter) who took an immense interest in my practice and to whom I wrote weekly with detailed accounts of my case. She preserved them and eventually handed some of them back to me in case I wanted to re-read them. I have tried to wade through them but with one or two exceptions have failed to find references to cases I wished to recall. I am sure that no barrister can remember all the cases in which he has appeared although some always remain in his memory. Sometimes I can recall the facts of cases without being sure whether I was in them or just sitting in court listening to them.

For example, the case of the resident gardener who worked fully clothed in a nudist colony. One night his clothes were burnt in a fire so he stole some of the nudists' clothes to cover his nakedness. And that of a youth who broke into a house one morning, was surprised, eluded his pursuers and hid himself in a wood. Hours later when he thought it was safe to do so he made his way to a road and thumbed a lift from a motorist. What he did not know until too late was that the driver was a police officer in plain clothes who had just come from making investigations at the house the youth had broken into, recognised him from the description he had received and drove him straight into the police station yard. Another case was of more dramatic content. In the night a householder heard noises indicating that someone had broken into the house. He told his wife to remain in bed, went downstairs and encountered the burglar. They became locked in a violent struggle. The wife, hearing alarming sounds, came downstairs. She was a very small woman and the burglar was exceedingly tall so she picked up the large torch he had dropped, drew up a chair beside the struggling pair, stood on it and hit the burglar exceedingly hard on the head with his torch. He fell to the ground but in order to make sure that he did not rise and attack again she hit him on the arm with the torch. Medical examination subsequently revealed that she had fractured his skull and his arm. He was a long time in hospital. At the trial the Judge said that he found it difficult to know how to deal with him but thought that perhaps he had been punished enough and bound him over.

There are other cases which stand out in my memory and in which I know I was concerned. One of these was in 1941 before the late Mr Justice Stable. I had to defend a man charged with obtaining board and lodging at a hospital by false pretences. The facts which emerged were that the defendant was skilled in bandaging one of his arms or legs and having done so, lay down by a roadside towards evening until some kindly motorist stopped and, at his request, drove him to hospital, There he explained that earlier in the day he had been run into by a car. When the doctor wished to examine the injured limb he appeared to be very distressed, saying that the wound had been dressed by a doctor at his surgery earlier in the day and that as the injury had now stopped hurting, could it please be left until morning before the dressing was removed and an examination made. This had worked on previous occasions and early the following morning he had recovered his clothing and slipped out of the hospital. But this time the doctors were too quick for him and uncovered his uninjured limb. Wearing my robes I saw my client in the cells on the morning of the trial. He was a white-haired, blue-eyed, apple-cheeked old darling to look at. Butter would not have melted in his mouth. He insisted on calling me 'Sister' and the burden of his instructions was that he would have to plead guilty but would I please do my best to persuade the Judge not to send him to prison but to send him to a hostel. He kept on saying "Oh sister, I am such a silly old man. I am so sorry for what I have done. I'll never do it again. Please help me". I swallowed this. It was not until I heard prosecuting counsel opening the case that I learned that he had committed the earlier similar offences. When his criminal record was read out, it included five cases of attempted suicide, at which the Judge remarked "Five! He cannot have been trying!" Of course he had not, this was another means of obtaining free board and lodging. The sentence was 18 months' imprisonment whereat what I can only describe as an explosion occurred in the dock: there was a stream of invective against the Judge and it took four prison officers to overpower the man and take him down the dock steps, still shouting abuse. I was horrified and being still rather green feared that the Judge would somehow hold me to blame after my earnest expression of my client's repentance and desire to reform. I think that Mr Justice Stable observed my discomfiture for a few minutes later his clerk brought me a note (which I still have) inviting me to dine at The Judges' Lodgings – my first of those cherished invitations to a member of the junior Bar. Underneath the signature was written "I was much pained at the aspersions your lay client cast at my parents' memory. To the best of my belief they were untrue." This was the start of my enduring and affectionate admiration for Mr Justice Stable.

Not many of the judges were given nicknames by the Bar but Mr Justice Stable was always known as 'Owlie' because of his habit of blinking. He was well aware of this and certainly did not resent it. Much later on I had letters from him in which he so signed himself. He was a very humane and shrewd criminal judge. As far as I know no book has ever been written recording the many true stories about him. It is not for me to attempt to remedy this but there are some anecdotes which I will recount. A poacher, who had poached the same land for years, was startled one day to hear the sound of a gun at a time when no landowner or gamekeeper was likely to be shooting. Investigation revealed that it was a young, interloping poacher who had been firing. The old boy warned him very seriously not to do it again or he would "get both barrels". The young poacher did it again and got both barrels as he ran. It took the hospital a long time to extract all the shot from the backs of his legs. The old boy pleaded guilty to wounding. Mr Justice Stable, who was himself a landowner, obviously felt a certain sympathy for him and bound him over for two years on condition that he did not carry a gun during that period. Asked if he understood the old boy said that he did, but when he was half-way down the dock steps Mr Justice Stable said, "Bring him back. He has not understood what I meant." Then, addressing him: "Listen to me. What I have said means that if, as I suppose, you intend to go on earning your living in the only way you know, for the next two years you will have to use NETS."

In a civil action the facts were that a little boy had suddenly run across the road in front of an oncoming lorry, giving the driver no opportunity to avoid running over him. The little boy's legs were gravely and permanently injured. I was instructed to settle the statement of claim but at first refused to do so because, on the evidence available, this action could not succeed. However, I received further instructions that the boy's father insisted on proceeding for reasons which I was given. This time reluctantly, I settled the statement of claim and conducted the case in court before Mr Justice Stable. The outcome was inevitable: judgment for the defendant with costs. The Judge was displeased with me and asked me why on earth I had brought such a hopeless case. I felt that I was at liberty to tell him that I had advised against bringing the claim but that the father had insisted on doing so in order that, later on, he could explain to his crippled son that he had taken all possible steps to recover compensation for him. The Judge looked very thoughtful and said something to the effect that now he understood and then, looking hard at counsel for the defence, said that the defendant (ie the insurers) need not enforce the costs unless it was desired to do so. I feel pretty sure that counsel would have asked his instructing solicitor to make it clear to the insurers that the Judge did not want the order for costs (which had had to be made in the circumstances) to be enforced.

Mr Justice Stable could be somewhat unconventional at times. I was once making my final speech in a civil action when his clerk came into court and whispered something to him. The Judge held up his hand and said, "One moment please. I have an announcement to make. By some horrible mischance the wrong horse has won the Derby." (He named the winner but I have forgotten it.)

In a criminal case I prosecuted a young Arab. He pleaded guilty but was said not to know any English so an interpreter had to be called to stand beside him in the dock and translate the proceedings. After a while Mr Justice Stable ordered the interpreter to leave the dock as the defendant could understand English perfectly well. At the time I thought this was rather high-handed but after the defendant had been put on probation I was outside the court when I heard him chatting away to the probation officer in fluent English. I asked Mr Justice Stable afterwards how he had known and the answer was "by watching the Defendant's eyes."

Finally, one more criminal case tried by Mr Justice Stable in May 1944. I appeared for the defence of two fine, upstanding young soldiers charged with robbery with violence. They were both parachutists (they were not called paratroopers then), and the circumstances were such that they had to plead guilty. They had been in a public house with their two girl-friends: also present was an American soldier who made a considerable display of his well-stuffed wallet and tried to entice one of the girls away from her soldier boy, about whom he

made derogatory remarks. No doubt all of them had had
plenty to drink when, later on, the parachutists crossed
the public house yard to the lavatory. On the way they
met the American soldier and one of the parachutists
felled him with a single blow. He fell face downwards
and his wallet could be seen protruding from his hip-
pocket. The parachutists took it. Now in 1944 the Amer-
icans were of course our allies although the conduct of
some of them did not always meet with universal
approval here and the discrepancy between their rates of
military pay and ours caused a certain amount of ill-
feeling. It was clear that in this case the American had
'asked for it' but it would have been wholly improper for
counsel in open court to make the kind of disparaging
criticisms which would have been permissible if the
victim had been British. I had to choose my words very
carefully but it was essential that I make the picture and
the provocation clear to the Judge so that he would really
understand what had occurred. He did: the sentence on
each of them was nine strokes of the birch and one month
in prison. (As the Judge afterwards told me – "Just long
enough for the marks of the birching to disappear.")
When the case was over I had to go down to the cells to
see another prisoner and while down there thought I
would have a word with the parachutists. I was appalled
at the change in them: one of them had obviously been
crying, the hair of the other had fallen down over his eyes
and he was hardly able to speak. He took a step towards
me in such an apparently menacing way that a prison
officer also took a step forward to intervene. One of them
started to say, "You . . . you . . ." and could get no
further. I thought that I was about to learn some new
words. I said briskly "It's only the birch you know, not
the cat." But I had misunderstood their feelings and
when he found his voice again he said, "Birch? Birch?
What the hell do we care about the birch? We thought we
were going to get three years and we've only got a
month. You're the best friend I've ever had in my life.

73

Now we shall be out in time for the big show". This was shortly before D-Day and the Normandy landing. They would not have been released in time for the initial landing but no doubt saw action soon afterwards. I have often wondered if they survived.

My practice was mainly on circuit and was a mixed one. The same solicitors often sent one their criminal, civil and divorce cases. It was essentially a common law practice, I only found myself uneasily in the Chancery Division on a couple of occasions. This was very much what I wanted. I certainly did not want a mainly criminal practice. In 1960 when I took Silk a provincial newspaper report described me as "one of the best known criminal barristers in England". Flattering, but inaccurate and I certainly did not wish to be known mainly as a criminal practitioner. I did hardly any criminal work in London mostly because in my early days Paul Sandlands told me not to go to the Central Criminal Court (the Old Bailey) or to London Sessions. Things have changed but in those days those Courts did not enjoy the high reputation they have today. One of the most derogatory remarks one could make about a barrister was that he was 'an Old Bailey hack'. I did make a few visits to the Central Criminal Court one of which was for an astonishingly high fee, but in general criminal work was badly paid. That is another thing which has changed radically, the fees for prosecuting have increased greatly and, particularly with legal aid, defending can be very profitable.

Down a mine

My principal interest was always in civil work. I never specialised in any branch of the law but one form of action which I found quite absorbing was common law claims arising out of accidents in coal mines. I did a lot of work for the Derbyshire branch of the National Union of Mineworkers. This, I suppose, was an unlikely kind of work for a woman barrister: it came about by chance.

Before he took Silk, the late Norman Winning was a well-known and most able junior on the Midland Circuit. He had done the work for the Derbyshire miners for a long time but on one occasion he was tied up in another court and could not take a case which was coming on the next day at Derbyshire Assizes. He suggested to the solicitor (who used to brief me in other cases) that I should take it on. All went well and then Norman suggested that, as he was over-burdened with written work, I should be instructed to do the opinions and pleadings. It ended up with my having the hearing briefs as well. When the mines were nationalised I found the National Coal Board much readier to settle cases than the private owners had been. This may have been a matter of policy.

As I did more of the work it became increasingly necessary that I should go down a coalmine. The N.C.B. solicitor demurred: the men would not like it, a woman down the pit was unlucky and so on. However, having signed a form absolving the Coal Board from any liabilities whatsoever, down I went, albeit during a maintenance shift, at Markham No 1 Colliery. This was very deep and ranked as a high hazard pit where the air pressure was double the normal and the temperature 80°F. Some four hours later I emerged, greatly dehydrated, and thankful to drink eight bottles of lemonade one after another in the manager's office. I was unbelievably dirty, my blackened face streaked with the grey stone-dust used to keep down the coal-dust. For obvious reasons, I could not use the pit-head baths and the best that could be found was a nailbrush and carbolic soap in the canteen manageress's cloakroom. Not recommended for the complexion. It had been a fascinating experience and two odd sensations remain in my memory: the certainty, when the cage was about halfway down the shaft, that we were travelling upwards and, with lamps extinguished when I was being shown by the under-manager how to test for gas, the darkness had a positive quality I had never known above ground, as though one were looking at black velvet held before one's eyes. I was not an apt pupil: when I was being taught how to test for 'drummy' (ie potentially unsafe) roof I got it wrong nearly every time. At one stage we went a considerable distance (it seemed like miles) under a 3 feet 6 inches high roof in a squatting position, I was certain that I was keeping my head down but again and again my helmet crashed against the roof.

When I reached the hotel where I was staying and was well-known, the hall porter on seeing me said, "Round to the back you!" It took four baths and four shampoos to get clean again. The following morning on arriving at the Court the Coal Board solicitor enquired anxiously whether I was all right, as his assistant, who had been sent with me to act as chaperon, was in hospital suffering from exhaustion. I feigned astonishment: I did not tell him that I ached in every limb and every muscle.

Murder

Although I preferred civil work, some criminal cases of course were very interesting. Before the abolition of the death penalty defending, or for that matter prosecuting, in a murder case was exceedingly anxious work. Silks were almost invariably briefed on both sides so the main responsibility rested on them, but the junior also had his share of anxiety. I have referred to the understanding and humanity of Mr Justice Stable but of course he was not the only judge with those qualities, for example there was the late Mr Justice Finnemore. He tried a most pathetic case of murder in which the facts were that a young, unmarried mother had thrown her 14-month-old child into the river where it drowned. She was of very low intelligence and had had a very unhappy life. There were other mitigating factors. She had done her best to care for the child in very difficult circumstances until the strain became too much for her and it was on a sudden impulse that she did what she did. If the child had been two or three months younger she might have been charged with the lesser offence of infanticide, or at least one could have hoped to obtain such a verdict, which of course did not carry the death penalty. As it was, the only possible defence was one of insanity. But no doctor had been found who was prepared to say that at the time of the offence she did not know the nature and quality of her act or, if she did, that she did not know that it was wrong. So for my leader and myself the task of defending her was unpleasantly like making bricks without straw. Mr Justice Finnemore could not have been more helpful to her in his summing-up. He pointed out that medical evidence was not necessary and that the jury could use their own common sense and experience in the light of the evidence they had heard. To no avail: the verdict was murder. With a white and horrified face the High Sheriff's chaplain moved to perform his obligatory task of placing the black cap on the Judge's head. Mr Justice Finnemore waved him away then, instead of pronouncing the mandatory long and spine-chilling words of the death sentence (". . . hanged by the neck until you are dead . . . and may the Lord have mercy on your soul.") he mumbled words to the effect that he was bound to sentence her to death but that perhaps she need not be too frightened. He then rose abruptly, went straight to the telephone in his retiring room and told the then Home Secretary that he wanted a reprieve for the girl by the next morning. And so it was. I suppose that one could say that judges ought not to break the rules, but how right he was! My leader sent me down to the cells to see the girl and try to reassure her. I was not at liberty to tell her in terms that she would not hang (and I did not know then what a prompt step the Judge had taken) but I had to tell her that in no circumstances must she appeal as this would only delay a reprieve (though I could not put it quite like that). I remember how furious I was with a woman prison officer who should have known better but who refused to let me see this girl because she was a prisoner under sentence of death, and that was what the rules said. I was still robed and counsel should be allowed access to their clients whatever the sentence. I sent for the principal prison officer who of course admitted me to the cell immediately.

After peace returned

In 1946 an ex-soldier named Holmes was charged with murdering his wife. Paul Sandlands and I were instructed to defend him. I went with our instructing solicitor to see him in Lincoln prison. He was the only man on a capital charge whom I have ever known to forbid his counsel to run a defence of insanity (not that I think that this would have been available). He said, and he meant it, that he would rather hang than be confined in a lunatic asylum. The defence was one of provocation by his wife's confession of adultery. It failed: he was convicted of murder and sentenced to death before the late Mr Justice Charles. An appeal to the Court of Criminal Appeal was dismissed. My leader and I were both dissatisfied with the trial and the way in which the appeal had been dismissed. Our complaint was not that he ought necessarily to have been convicted of manslaughter and not murder, but that the Judge had failed to leave the decision fairly to the jury and that the Court of Criminal Appeal ought to have so held (there was no question on the facts of his being found not guilty of either offence). Two days before the date fixed for the execution the necessary fiat was given and we appealed to the House of Lords. The newspapers made a good deal of the fact that this was the first time a woman barrister had appeared in the House of Lords in a murder appeal. The opposition was somewhat weighty: Sir Frank Soskice K.C. who was the Solicitor General (afterwards Lord Stow Hill), Anthony Hawke (afterwards Common Serjeant of the City of London) and Rodger

Winn (afterwards Lord Justice Winn). None of them is alive today. Paul Sandlands of course made the opening speech for the appellant and I followed with a second and shorter one. The case for the Crown was concluded on the fourth day of the hearing which left the reply for the appellant to be made on the following day. At that time Paul Sandlands was Recorder of Birmingham and his Quarter Sessions were due to start on the following day. He felt that he had to be there and he asked their Lordships to excuse his further attendance and to permit his junior to continue the case for the appellant. This was a more or less unheard of request in a murder appeal in the House of Lords, but it was granted. So I made the speech in reply. The appeal was dismissed and I think that Paul Sandlands had realised that this was almost bound to happen. Their Lordships deferred giving their reasons to a later date and these were not given until after Holmes had been hanged. As a last resort I had made written representations to the then Home Secretary for a reprieve, but in vain. The case was reported in the Law Reports and became the leading authority that mere words cannot amount to provocation such as to reduce murder to manslaughter, at any rate until the passing of the Homicide Act of 1957.

First appointment

In 1948 came my first official appointment. This was as a member of a Home Office Committee of Enquiry, chaired by the late Mr Justice Byrne, into the use of Depositions in Criminal Cases. The recommendation was strongly in favour of their retention in committal proceedings. I have no doubt that this was right at that period, but it was a time-consuming process and the immense increase in the number of criminal cases led to the procedure being changed and now reliance can be placed on written statements in preliminary proceedings.

Exercising judicial duties

In 1953 Paul Sandlands wished me to sit as an assistant Recorder of Birmingham. He had to obtain the approval of the Lord Chancellor who at first demurred: no woman had ever been so appointed before and so on. But Paul was very persuasive and so I duly sat: my first exercise of judicial duties. I was in a fine old state of nerves on the first day but thereafter became less apprehensive and more and more interested in doing the work. There was already one assistant, another member of the junior Bar and as Birmingham had the peculiarity of holding six Quarter Sessions in a year, it was much better for our practices at the Bar that we should sit in turn so that neither of us should be absent from our normal work too often. The pressure of the Birmingham case-load was such that we often sat until 6.00 or 7.00 p m. Later the number of assistants was increased.

I have no idea of whether this is still the case, almost certainly not, but in my day Birmingham was known in some circles as 'the University of Crime'. This was because promising young London criminals were sent there for further education in their chosen profession and had the advantage that they would be unknown to the police there. This was not always the case. I remember a member of the C.I.D. telling me that there had been a 'tip-off' that one such 'undergraduate' would be travelling to Birmingham on a particular train. His name and a full description of him enabled two officers to meet and identify him. They greeted him by name (always an advantage to the police) and said that they did not think that he would like Birmingham, told him that there was a train leaving for London at such a time and handed him a single ticket to take him back. He went.

There was a most efficient shorthand writer in the court in which I sat. He knew the procedure as well as any trained court official and was very helpful to judicial beginners. A whispered aside to a new assistant recorder (or for that matter to an experienced one who might momentarily forget) "Does the defendant want to ask the witness any questions?" or "Does he want to call any witnesses?" could save one from an omission which might have resulted in a successful appeal in an otherwise unmeritorious case.

Mainly the cases at Quarter Sessions were what lawyers call 'run-of-the-mill'; endless stealing and receiving offences, punctuated by those of driving under the influence of drink, indecent assault, and so on. Some of the cases of course were of particular interest and several of these stand out clearly in my recollection, they were all pleas of guilty. I will refer later to defended cases in general, not specifically related to Birmingham.

The youngest offenders I ever dealt with in any court appeared at Birmingham Quarter Sessions charged with burglary. They were two boys of about 11 years old who would certainly have been dealt with by a juvenile court for a less serious offence. During the hours of darkness they had broken into the house of an old lady and stolen, I think, her purse. She was very seriously upset by the burglary, could no longer sleep properly and was afraid to go out alone. Both boys came from good homes in the village where the old lady lived and neither had been in trouble before. I decided either to bind them over or put them on probation, I cannot remember which. Having announced my decision I explained to them in some detail the harm they had done to the old lady and said that while I could not make this part of my order, it would probably be a comfort to her if they spent their next pocket money on a bunch of flowers and took it to her and said that they were sorry. It seemed to me that if she could see for herself how small her burglars were it might help to assuage her fears. In response to this suggestion one of them gave me a sneering look and was certainly not going to comply, but the other one did as I suggested and I learned afterwards that it had been of considerable effect in allaying her anxieties.

There is a sharp distinction to be drawn between breaking into uninhabited premises such as a factory and housebreaking, particularly burglary, of occupied residences. Too often the greatest harm done in the latter is not the stealing of property but the terror which the incursion causes to the inhabitants, especially to those who are either young or old. I am sure that everyone would agree that one of the most lamentable features of present day crime is the frequency with which the old and the helpless are attacked. The old-fashioned pickpockets and bag-snatchers seem to me to have been paragons of good behaviour compared with the modern muggers and other thieves who use violence not only to obtain their loot but also because, so it seems, they must obtain satisfaction from the infliction of pain. On those criminals I would have no mercy at all.

Among the early cases which came before me at Birmingham was that of two men, probably in their late fifties, who had broken into a sports pavilion and stolen food from the canteen. They could be described as 'old lags', each with a string of convictions as long as your arm. Although it was a comparatively minor offence it seemed at first that, in view of their records, sentences of preventive detention (a form of punishment since abolished) would be appropriate. They had left prison together a few days before the offence. Neither of them was represented; one had virtually nothing to say for himself but the other had a good deal to say. He told me that while serving his last sentence he had definitely decided to have done with crime and to look after his wife who had had to suffer because of his absences in gaol. This was not an unfamiliar story but he went on to say that he had so informed Detective Inspector Quinn (I think and hope that I have correctly remembered the name and rank), who had believed him and told him that if he found himself in difficulty after his discharge he was to come and see him. He added "Fool that I was not to do as he said" and explained that he and the other man had

Dame Elizabeth at about 6 months old – with 'Wagger'

Lindsay in 1910

Aged about 7. With Father and Rushton

Aged about 7

Father in Switzerland, 1913

Mother in about 1921

Randall in about 1933

About 1965

Randall at Asolo, Italy, 1974

Lindsay in Switzerland, 1983

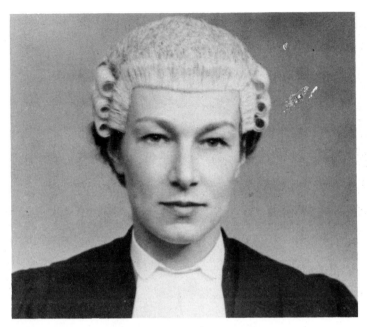

At the Bar in about 1945

In Silk, 1960

County Court Judge, 1962

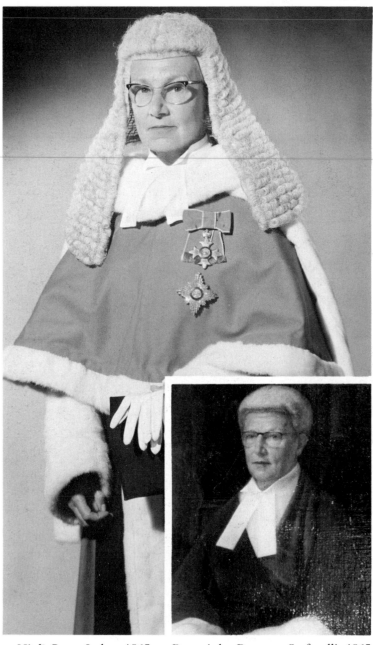

High Court Judge, 1965   Portrait by Romano Stefanelli, 1965

At Westminster Abbey for the Annual Service
on the opening day of the Michaelmas Sittings, about 1972

Working, 1965

spent the money which they had been given on discharge and were very hungry when they broke in. On this, I asked for Detective Inspector Quinn to come into the witness box. He confirmed what the prisoner had said and added that as a very experienced police officer he had heard many protestations of reform which had not impressed him but that this time, surprisingly, in spite of the man's record, he had believed him. He further added that if only he had come to see him, he would have given him money out of his own pocket rather than that he should slip back into crime. This was food for thought indeed. I asked for the senior probation officer to be called into the witness-box and then asked him if he knew the two men in the dock. He did indeed! I do not of course know what went through his mind but I would hazard a guess that it was near unbelief that anyone could be so crazy as to put such men on probation and perhaps a reflection that this just showed how unsuitable a woman was to exercise judicial functions. I put both men on probation for three years. When I adjourned I asked the probation officer to see me in my room. I then explained what had transpired before he came into court and asked him not to bother with the first man who would probably commit another offence within six weeks (I think that it turned out to be only three weeks) but to do all he could for the other one. This was a challenge to which he responded. There was an excellent arrangement at Birmingham Quarter Sessions that every time one came back to sit there one was given a list of the defendants one had earlier put on probation and a report on their progress. Each time I saw the list thereafter I scanned it with trepidation but growing relief. The man did not offend again but got a job and was doing his best to make up to his loyal wife for all the suffering he had caused her. That was the best order I ever made in any criminal case. It was only made possible by the conduct of the detective inspector. He was by no means the only police officer I came across who helped a convicted criminal, but he is one whom I shall not forget.

In another case there was a daring night theft from a factory where a lorry loaded with metal was taken from a locked loading bay inside the premises. The two thieves had concealed themselves in the factory during the day. They had ascertained that there was an elderly indoor night-watchman who always cooked himself a meal and then, so they had been informed, invariably went to sleep with his keys near to hand. Sure enough he cooked his supper that night and they waited for him to fall asleep. But he did not do so. Hour after hour passed and he was still very much awake. It was essential to the successful commission of the crime that the lorry be driven out and well away from the factory before dawn. It was not until they were beginning to lose hope that, at last, the watchman fell asleep. They were able to take the keys and drive away the lorry undetected, although some time later they were arrested. They were unrepresented at the trial and I do not recall what, if any, previous convictions they had but this was hardly the crime of first offenders. When I envisaged the scene, with two strong young men watching the old man, almost endlessly as it must have seemed to them, it struck me that the temptation to use violence and 'put him to sleep' must have been very strong. But they were not prepared to do so and were ready to abandon the theft first. It seemed to me that this was so much in their favour that I gave them very light sentences, without saying why.

Violence

The last case illustrates the difference between many of those who committed this kind of crime 30 years ago and many of those who do so today. In the present climate of violence one could hardly hope for such restraint as those two men exercised. Social scientists and others seem to me to have failed to come up with any explanation, let alone any solution, of the modern epidemic of violence in criminal activities. In earlier days there were many men prepared to take part in serious offences but only on condition that no member of the gang carried a gun or other offensive weapon. Presumably there are still some of the same mind, but if statistics are any guide, they are comparatively few in number. It makes one smile wryly to re-read what the late Sir Travers Humphreys wrote in 1945 after his retirement from the High Court Bench:

"The armed burglar today is almost extinct and has been replaced by the slim athlete who can swarm up a drainpipe and remove a pane of glass without noise."★

How times have changed! Perhaps the modern plastic drainpipe, which would probably collapse under the weight of even a slim climber, has contributed to the virtual disappearance of the cat-burglar.

Further on the subject of violence I agree with the view that films, videos and television programmes depicting violence make a substantial contribution to present attitudes, particularly of the young, but this is obviously not the whole explanation. No doubt many people would disagree with me, but I believe another factor to be the abolition of the death penalty. It would of course be ridiculous to suggest that fear of hanging was an unfailing deterrent to murderers or those who carried weapons with which murder might be committed. But it seems to me that since the abolition of the death penalty in 1965 the respect for human life has markedly diminished. It is my view that the most potent effect of the death penalty was not at the time of planning or committing the offence but years earlier when the young were growing up and adults living in the knowledge that murder was so heinous a crime that the State itself took away the life of the murderer. This I believe engendered a respect for human life, not the reverse as some would argue. I do not suggest that my contention of itself is anything like a sufficient reason for restoring the death penalty and of course I

★*Criminal Days*, p 51 (Hodden and Stoughton, 1946).

recognise that there are weighty arguments against its restoration. And I must acknowledge that if the penalty were restored it might be years before any effect in reducing the number of murders would become apparent. Time would have to elapse while the young grew to maturity, for it is surely during the formative years that the respect of human life can be fostered. However, it is perhaps idle to speculate too much on the might-have-been when it is probable that for the foreseeable future the death penalty is dead.

No doubt what more I say on the subject of violence today will be disputed, perhaps, angrily, in some quarters: I believe that the lack of Christian belief is the main cause. So many parents nowadays are devoid of such belief, in consequence their own conduct suffers and even more so does that of their children. One of the principal teachings of Christianity is respect for others, even if it is sometimes almost impossibly difficult to follow the precept that one should love one's enemies. True one does not have to be a Christian to respect other people but it is probably easier and at the same time more compelling for Christians to do so than for those without belief.

Another principal factor is the lack of discipline in the home, which is probably more prevalent in non-religious households. I am firmly of the view that sensible disciplines makes for happy childhood and that lack of reasonable restraint on their behaviour leaves children feeling insecure – like being on a staircase without banisters. A feeling of insecurity breeds discontent and sometimes bad behaviour may be indulged in as an unconscious means of assuaging the feeling. A suitable rebuke or punishment may serve to reassure a child.

Further, while nobody in his senses would deny the immense benefits bestowed by the Welfare State, it does seem to me that one of its disadvantages is to damage the feeling of parental responsibility and pride. Once upon a time the father knew himself to be head of the family.

This is much less the case in larger sections of the public today: he no longer feels the old responsibility to provide for and bring up his children: the State does it for him. So let the schools discipline and train the young and the State keep them all if necessary! And if father has less responsibility the children will probably treat him with less respect. On the other hand the over-disciplined young of the Victorian heavy father were not infrequently provoked to rebelliousness. It is by no means easy always to find the happy mean.

In saying all this I do not underestimate the unhappy lot of the all-too-numerous fathers who are unemployed today. Other people have written more eloquently than I could about the evils of unemployment but none of these evils seems to me to be more cruel than the loss of one's self-respect. To be unwanted is surely one of the most hurtful of all feelings. I have profound sympathy for the difficulty an unemployed man may face in trying to bring up his children properly. At the same time it seems to me that the jobless who take to crime, particularly of a violent kind cannot rely on their unemployment as an infallible excuse. There was extensive unemployment in this country at the beginning of this century, which virtually disappeared during the 1914–18 war only to rear its ugly head again afterwards, culminating in the depression of the 1930s with about three million unemployed. Further there was much greater poverty than there is now and, allowing for inflation, the unemployed are now far better supported financially than in the earlier period. Yet the crime rate during those hard times did not soar and violent behaviour was far less in evidence.

It is a melancholy but all too obvious fact that even the best of homes may produce young who commit offences. So often I have had the very sad experience of listening to a parent in the witness-box, shocked and bewildered by a son's misdeeds, saying "He has always been a good boy at home". One hears talk today about 'peer pressure' but often juvenile delinquency seems to me to be more a case of 'He does it so why shouldn't I? than of 'He does it so I must'. Bad behaviour is like an infectious disease – some catch it and some do not and the immunisation of a good home is not always effective. All this is generalisation and bristles with exceptions, but I cannot find other explanations for the present sorry state of law-breaking.

Strikes

Mention of violence in these days makes one think of the miners' strike. There were strikes before I was born and have been ever since, some of which involved violence on both sides of the dispute. But in the old days workmen sometimes had no alternative but to strike when they were paid pitifully inadequate wages and needed unions to support their reasonable claims. We need unions but the change which I have witnessed and deplored is the excessive power which they have acquired by subjecting a majority of their fellow-citizens to great distress and hardship.

The latest miners' strike is the worst example of this, even though its aim to paralyse the country was thwarted by the successful meaures taken to maintain power supplies. The prime object of the strike seems to be widely recognised now as political, i e to bring down the democratically elected Government which in the present session and the preceding one had a mandate to curb the excessive powers of the unions.

Lord Stockton (formerly Mr Harold Macmillan) said in his maiden speech in the House of Lords in 1984 that the miners' strike "breaks my heart". Many of us know how he felt. I had had enough contact with miners professionally to make me admire and respect them for their skill and courage and their loyalty to each other. Loyalty is one thing but the kind of intimidation, brutality and even murder aimed against their own mates which we have witnessed is something altogether different.

Before the 1974–5 strike I used to be puzzled by the football hooligans and wondered what made those who seemed, in general, to be otherwise decent enough lads, seek to injure each other for no better reason than their support of a particular club. The sad answer given by the strike seems to be that the propensity for this kind of violence is latent in thousands of apparently respectable men. This of course is not to suggest that every striking miner has used violence or intimidation, many have not done so or even joined in picketing. Perhaps indeed the proclivity is innate in most men, if so, where have we gone wrong in creating a society in which the impulse to violence is no longer restrained as it used to be?

So much has already been said and written about the miners' strike that I will refrain from commenting further on it save for two matters, first to express my own respect and admiration for the immense courage and determination of those miners who have continued to exercise their right to work. They have lessened the disgrace brought on the nation by the conduct of many others of the strikers and their leaders. Second, to say that I wish that Arthur Scargill and his officials would answer one question: why should miners who are already highly paid in a heavily subsidised industry expect, or be entitled to, far more favourable treatment at the expense of the taxpayer than workers in any other industry, whether nationalised or not? In private industry or business, for example, if redundancies are commercially necessary, redundancy payments are normally made out of the profits which the employees have made by their work for their employers. This is very far from being the case in the mining industry.

Criminal defences

Now I come back to criminal defences.

Defended cases can of course be absorbingly interesting but a good many of them can be pretty dull. Sometimes when trying cases I used to think how unimaginative some defendants were and that, if they were going to lie, how much better a job they could have made of it. As defending counsel the palpably unimpressive nature of the defence often struck one. But of course not the slightest suggestion or hint could be given to the defendant as to how to improve it. It is for him to put forward his defence, not for counsel to tinker with it. If a defendant admits to counsel in conference that he is guilty then he cannot be put into the witness-box to deny it. To do so would be a gross breach of a barrister's duty not to mislead the court. If a defendant insists that he wishes to deny his guilt in the witness-box despite his admission then the barrister must refuse to act further for him. Nevertheless, as every man is entitled to have the case proved against him before he can be convicted, in some instances one may allow him to plead not guilty and let the prosecution prove its case if it can, but call no evidence for the defence.

People are better informed nowadays about criminal procedure but formerly it was quite common for a barrister to be asked how he could defend a case when he must realise that his client is guilty: the answer is quite simple: in the absence of an admission of guilt it is no part of a barrister's business to decide whether his client is guilty, that is for the decision of the jury under the guidance of the judge. It is, however, permissible and proper for a barrister to advise a defendant that, on the evidence available, he is almost certain to be convicted and to advise him to plead guilty. But the decision is always that of the defendant. A judge is likely to form a better opinion of a defendant who is man enough, and sensible enough, to admit his guilt than for one who tells a pack of lies and is then convicted.

One of what I may call the 'standard' defences to a charge of receiving stolen goods (which is now handling

stolen goods) used to be, and I daresay still is, that the
goods were bought from a man met in a public house: his
surname was always unknown but if he had a first name it
was invariably a very common one. This defence was
generally considered by counsel for the prosecution (or
for the defence) as being, perhaps, not a non-starter, but
an unlikely winner. My memory may be at fault but I
cannot recall a single acquittal in such a case.

The offence in which there was most likely to be an
acquittal when common sense should have dictated a
conviction was driving after drinking too much. It used
to be unkindly said among lawyers that this was due to a
fellow-feeling for the defendant on the part of some of
the jurors. Nowadays the breath-test and other analyses
have helped to put a rightful conviction beyond doubt. In
one case I tried at Birmingham, before these modern
inventions, the prosecution suggested to the defendant
that the large quantity of whisky which he admitted
drinking was enough to make any man tipsy but he
maintained that this was no more than his daily con-
sumption and that it had not affected him at all. It was put
to him that although he was drinking he had had nothing
to eat all day; he denied this and when he was asked what
he had eaten the answer was "Whelks". He was convicted. (There was other evidence against him.)

One method adopted by some criminals, if circumstances allow, is to follow the Napoleonic precept that
attack is the best form of defence and to allege that one
of the prosecution witnesses committed the offence.
This form of defence is fraught with peril. Broadly
speaking it can only be used if either the defendant has
no previous convictions, or only minor ones such as are
unlikely to damage his credibility, or alternatively if the
prosecution witness has admittedly played some part in
the commission of the offence. The necessity for caution
is because ordinarily a defendant's past convictions are
concealed from the jury, but if he attacks the character
of a prosecution witness (and in some other specified

circumstances) his previous convictions can be disclosed. This is on the equitable principle that if the pot calls the kettle black, the kettle can call the pot black. Where a defendant's earlier convictions are not disclosed until after the jury has returned a verdict of guilty and his record is then read out before sentence is passed, one may sometimes see a look of astonishment or bewilderment on the faces of the jurors. Some of them, I believe, feel that it is unfair that they should not be told before verdict what kind of man they are trying. But the better view is that it would be unfair to the accused man that the jury should start by being prejudiced against him because of his past record. Nowadays juries are growing more knowing and some of them realise that if evidence of the defendant's good character is not given it is probably because there is something to hide.

To give an example of the Napoleonic defence, in 1952 I defended two men on a charge of office-breaking and stealing. The offence took place at the office of a large dairy company: the safe was opened with an oxyacetylene torch and over £6,000 stolen. They had learned the lay-out of the office building and the position and type of the safe from a cashier formerly employed by the company. He knew why they wanted the information and expected to receive a 'cut' from the proceeds. Afterwards, although a man of previously good character, he committed other offences and then left for France and joined the Foreign Legion, but not before receiving his 'cut'. Some time later his admirable wife persuaded him to return and to confess his crimes to the police. He was prosecuted and dealt with for the other offences. The defence of the two defendants was that he had committed the safe-breaking and that they had had nothing to do with it. The prosecution was obliged to call the ex-cashier as a witness but as he was admittedly an accomplice and himself gave evidence of his other offences, the criminal records of the two defendants were not disclosed before verdict. The ex-cashier's wife gave evidence of having seen them bringing money to the house for him and as she was anything but an accomplice they admitted this but gave unconvincing explanations for it. The ex-cashier's somewhat melodramatic departure for the Foreign Legion afforded me considerable scope for cross-examination and in addressing the jury but both men were convicted.

Sometimes an accomplice may agree with his fellow-defendants to take the whole blame for the offence. One such was a 'greyhound ringing' case in 1946 in which I prosecuted with the assistance of a junior. Three men were charged with conspiracy to defraud by entering a first-class runner in a race under the name of a poor runner. The two animals were reasonably alike but some discrepancies in colouring were concealed before the race by one of the conspirators who was a hairdresser. The supposed poor runner attracted the expectedly long odds, although bookmakers in various places were surprised that there was a rush of betting on it just before the race. It won. The defence was that the hairdresser was the only one involved and that as a man cannot conspire with himself all three should be acquitted. They were all three convicted and sentenced to nine months' hard labour. (The imposition of hard labour has since been abolished.) Although the trio had originally been charged also with the substantive offence of fraudulently obtaining the proceeds of the bets, it had not been possible to obtain sufficient evidence of the successful bets having been placed on behalf of any of them. So at the outset of the case I felt obliged to inform the Court that I should only proceed on the conspiracy charge. Until then the defendants would not have known that this was going to happen and it is a reasonable assumption that there had been an agreement that if the hairdresser alone were convicted of the substantive offence the other two would have compensated him in some way. This case had its moments: when I called for 'Exhibit 1', the door of the Court was opened and in dashed a greyhound dragging a policeman on a lead! Also, during the hearing the lights failed and the court was plunged into darkness, during which (as I later learned) a number of thefts took place and I was just able to make out a hand coming towards a gold pencil I had on the table before me. I grabbed the pencil just in time. I had no idea where the hand came from.

To continue with defences, there is of course our old friend the alibi. When I was a member of the Bar there was no obligation on the defence to disclose beforehand that an alibi was to be relied on at the trial. The first indication of this could come when defending counsel opened his case to the jury, although prosecuting counsel might guess what was coming from the kind of cross-examination of his witnesses: no challenge as to the facts of the case, only questions about the indentity of the offender. But even so, he might not be much wiser as to the nature of the alibi. Provided that the defence opening was fairly circumspect, the police could not check on the alibi until the defendant gave evidence, when it was probably too late to make enquiries at the public house, or wherever the defendant was said to have been at the material time. However, if the alibi was a really good one, the defence might choose to disclose it in some detail early enough for the prosecution to check on it before it was too late. Then if enquiries yielded no joy to the prosecution, defending counsel was in a strong position to point out to the jury that the prosecution were unable to contradict the defence evidence of the alibi. All this sparring came to an end when, in 1967, it was enacted that if an alibi was to be relied on, notice of this had to be given to the prosecution in time for the prosecution to investigate its accuracy.

Because cinema films are usually shown on successive days, an alibi that the accused man was at the cinema watching a particular film, of which he could give a detailed description, was incomplete unless he could adduce evidence that the cinema visit was on a date and at a time which would have made it impossible for him to be at the scene of the crime. Otherwise he could take the precaution of seeing the film a day or two before or after the offence was committed. As the same film is sometimes shown at more than one cinema, he needed supporting evidence of which cinema he attended. Nevertheless I have known an uncorroborated alibi of 'at the cinema' to succeed.

As television programmes are seldom repeated within a day or two an alibi of 'at home watching television' might be more difficult, except that modern science has made it possible to make one's own recording of broadcast programmes, but I have no experience of this happening.

An 'at work at the time' alibi may have a better chance of success but does not always succeed. In the 1940s I appeared for the prosecution in two or three cases against the same man. I remember him well. He was a very handsome man, but his record did not match his looks and various convictions were recorded against him. He was never represented as he preferred to conduct his own defence. In one case when I asked him an awkward question he shook his handsome head sadly and said "Ah, Madam, if only I had your education and eloquence!" I said "You need neither education nor eloquence to tell the Court where you were at. . ." and hoped thereby to nullify any sympathy he might undeservedly have aroused in the jury. In the case of the alibi, he was in work at the time as a chargehand engineer and on the day of the offence had clocked on at 7.00 p m. He did not remain at work until the shift ended. The prosecution were able to prove that for some time before 10.00 p m he and a workmate were drinking in a nearby public house. Just before 11.30 p m a police constable was walking along a road when he heard the sound of geese squawking. He shone his torch and saw Handsome, whom he recognised, and his mate. Handsome had a live goose draped round his neck, which he dropped before he struck the police officer, who closed with him. The mate picked up the goose and hit the constable with it and also hit him on the head with a bottle of beer. The goose died of the attack and the beer bottle broke but, though dazed, the constable managed to draw his truncheon and strike Handsome on the side of the head before the two men got away. They both went back to their place of work, but Handsome had to explain the cut on the side of his head, so he lay down beside a large metal vat, groaning loudly. When help came he explained that he had been working on top of the vat and caught his head on the corner of it as he fell. Unfortunately for the two defendants, their clothes were sent to a Home Office laboratory where goose feathers were found on them. Bye-bye alibi!

The evidence of a seemingly truthful witness that the defendant was in his company away from the scene of the crime at the material time can be most impressive. I remember prosecuting in one such case where the witness was a thoroughly reputable and patently honest man who had called at the defendant's house to collect an instalment payment or the like and found him and his family celebrating a good win on a horse. In the witness-box the witness was positive that this occurred on the evening of a particular race, an easily verifiable date which was in fact the evening when the crime was committed. Although there was prosecution evidence which incriminated the defendant, not surprisngly he was acquitted. With hindsight I suspected that the alibi witness had been mistaken and that what had happened was that the win being celebrated was on another race on another day. Admittedly, the defendant had been to see the witness some time after the event and asked him if he remembered calling at the time of the celebration of a win on, say, the Gold Cup at Ascot (I cannot remember which race meeting it was). The witness remembered it very well but, not being a racing man, he accepted from the defendant without question, and thought that he himself remembered, that the race was the Gold Cup,

96

whereas in fact it was, say, the Queen Elizabeth Stakes. If the alibi had been disclosed before the trial, as statute would have later required, I could have been instructed as to the dates of the two races and the witness could have been asked to check the date of the call with his records. Of course my suspicions might have been ill-founded and those records might have shown that the call took place on the day the Gold Cup race was run.

Where there is a genuine alibi and the police can check it before the trial this may lead to the charge being dropped or at any rate an innocent man being acquitted at his trial.

The best alibi of which I ever heard was that of a man who was able to have evidence called that prison records showed that at the time of the offence charged he was in prison for another offence and safely locked in his cell.

In Ireland there used to be what was called the 'Tipperary alibi' which consisted of calling witnesses to swear that at the material time not only was the defendant somewhere other than at the scene of the crime but so were all the prosecution witnesses. Very thorough, but I never knew it to be tried on in England.

One of the most anxious situations which may arise when one is performing judicial functions and has to sum-up is where, though it cannot be said that there is no evidence on which a jury could properly convict (which would result in the case being withdrawn from the jury), nevertheless one feels sure that the defendant is innocent. In those rather rare circumstances one can properly sum-up heavily in his favour, but the prosecution's case must also be put fairly. On the other hand, however certain one may be the defendant is guilty, the defence must always be given due weight. Juries are very conscious that it is their province to determine guilt or innocence and over-emphasis of the prosecution's case may result in a perverse acquittal. Years ago after such an acquittal one juror was heard to say to another "That'll teach the old so-and-so to try to dictate to us."

The jury's 'nose'

The care and attention which juries give to a case is something of which this nation can be proud. Inevitably juries vary, some are collectively intelligent, some are less so but many have what I call a 'nose' for guilt or innocence. As an example of this I take a case in which I was instructed to defend a salesman charged with embezzlement or fraudulent conversion. Part of his duty was to collect money from customers and to receipt the accounts. His books of accounts had carbon copies. Together with the money collected, the book was handed in to his employers' office at regular intervals. Another employee entered the amounts shown on the carbons in a ledger. It was discovered that in a number of instances the amounts shown on the copies were smaller than those on the top copies which were handed to the customer and correctly set out the amounts they had paid. One possible explanation was that the defendant had inserted a piece of paper under the carbon itself and filled in the amounts on the supposed copies afterwards. The defence was quite simply that he had used the book correctly and handed over all the money he had received. Asked if he could point to any other member of the staff who could have perpetrated the fraud, he said that he could not. It seemed almost ridiculous in the face of the evidence, but both my instructing solicitor and I believed him. In the witness-box there he stood, a man of irreproachable character, perfectly prepared to agree that the facts all pointed to his guilt but saying "I cannot explain it, I wish I could." The Judge appeared to be somewhat puzzled by the case but of course left it fairly to the jury. The defendant was acquitted. After the case ended and he had nothing more to gain he asked to see me. He said that now that it was all over he wanted to tell me again that he "had not done it". I have never known a case in which the facts looked so black against a defendant and yet I was so completely convinced that he was not guilty. Heaven be praised for such a perceptive jury!

Practice at the Bar with periodic exercise of judicial functions makes for an interesting life. Certainly I found it so. It meant hard, sometimes extremely hard, work with a good deal of pressure, but I was a very happy member of the junior Bar.

Chapter 8
In Silk

In 1958 I decided to apply for Silk. This is often a difficult decision to take and something of a gamble, although perhaps less so in recent times than it was in my day. There have been quite a number of successful juniors with large practices who have been failures as Queen's Counsel.

Before I made the decision I asked the advice of the late Mr Justice Geoffrey Lawrence who was then one of our ablest and most respected Silks. He advised that there were certain questions to ask oneself: "Am I doing the kind of case in which a leader would probably be briefed if I were not in it?" "Are my financial means such that I could manage if I did not succeed in Silk?" "Is there room for another Silk in my present Chambers, if not would I be prepared to move to others or to set up Chambers of my own?" The answers seemed to be "Yes" rather than "No", so my application to the Lord Chancellor was made. It failed. In those days apparently the practice was to give Silk to a certain number of those who practised on each of the circuits. I did not know until later that another Midland circuiteer, senior to me in call and circuit membership had also applied and would be likely to succeed if there were only one more Silk to be appointed on our circuit – unless I was made a special case. As I had always maintained that a woman at the Bar should be treated in exactly the same way as men it was unreasonable of me to be piqued when my application failed, but I was. My ruffled feathers were somewhat smoothed when a High Court judge, not one of the two whom I had asked to be referees in support of my application, told me that he had said to the Lord Chancellor of the day that my not getting Silk was "a bloody shame". In those days it was quite common for a first, or later, application to be turned down and everybody said that I must take the usual course and apply again in the following year. I did not do so, partly because of my unjustifiable pique and partly because I anticipated something of a bumper year ahead if I remained a junior. In 1960 I applied again and this time succeeded. I never regretted it.

I was by no means the first woman in Silk. In 1948 the first in Great Britain was that most able and charming member of the Scottish Bar Miss (now Dame) Margaret Kidd. In 1949 England had her first, two together, the late Mrs Helena Normanton and Miss Rose Heilbron (afterwards Mrs Justice Heilbron).

In order to ease the transition from being a junior to being in Silk, one could finish those cases in which one had already been instructed, without the necessity for a junior to be instructed as well. This was not only for the benefit of the new Silk but also in fairness to clients who did not wish to be deprived of their chosen counsel but would not want to instruct and pay for two.

The relief of having no new pleadings to draft and fewer opinions and advices to write was delightful. While nearly all new cases involved a good deal of work, there were working days when one could be missing from Chambers and do other things. It was a luxury during term-time to be able to shop at leisure instead of trying to cram everything into a Saturday morning when most of the London shops were shut in those days. Buying food was not one of my tasks because we always had a resident housekeeper, but there were all-important matters like a new hat requiring attention. One could even go to Wimbledon occasionally in the middle of the week instead of having to depend on Saturday tickets.

Having a good junior could be a great help. In a libel action in which I acted for the plaintiff there was no dispute that the document concerned was a most scurrilous libel, but the point at issue was its 'publication'. Libels written to the person libelled are not actionable provided that the writer does not communicate them to any one (apart from the writer's spouse) other than the recipient. My junior drew my attention to a particular authority which I had looked at and discarded as being insufficiently in point, but the enterprising junior (who is now a Circuit Judge) suggested a way in which use could be made of it which I gladly adopted as part of my argument. This being a libel action we exercised our right to have a jury at the trial. They found in our favour and fixed an appropriate amount of damages. The unsuccessful defendant appealed. In the Court of Appeal Gerald Gardiner Q.C. (afterwards Lord Gardiner and a Lord Chancellor) was briefed to lead for the appellant, a formidable advocate if ever there was one, but we managed to hold the judgment in favour of the plaintiff.

Another murder

In November 1960 I defended in a murder case in which there was little hope of avoiding a conviction. The accused man was a Pole, a butcher by trade, who had come here as a refugee from Nazi occupation and brutality. He was the mildest of men, as the local probation officer agreed, well liked in the English village where he lived and much loved by the local children to whom he was particularly kind. Yet one night he drank too much brandy and broke into the house of a woman who had earlier befriended him and let him lodge in the house. In his intoxicated state he went to sleep on the sitting room sofa. Early on the following morning the woman found him there, took hold of him and tried to rouse him. He sprang up and strangled her before, as he said, he was fully awake or conscious. No other defence being available it was necessary to rely on non-insane automatism and plead that what he did was an automatic reaction by a man not fully come to his senses and who had earlier lived in fear of sudden arrest and ill-treatment. In short, that his mind did not go with his deed. The defence, which as far as I know had never previously been used in a murder case, was made more difficult by the fact that later on the same morning when he must have been fully conscious he cut up and buried the body. We sought to attribute this to his continuing fear of arrest and imprisonment. Another and considerable difficulty was that, although a wallet containing money was found with the body in the grave he had dug, he took other money from the house and spent it locally. Yet another difficulty of a different kind was that at the trial although his knowledge of English was adequate he could not be persuaded to speak up when in the witness-box. Neither prosecuting counsel nor I could hear what he was saying and I do not think that the jury could either. The only person who could hear was the Judge, the witness-box being nearer to him than to anyone else. With infinite patience and care the late Mr Justice Havers (whose daughter is now a High Court Judge) repeated clearly everything that the defendant had said. The verdict was guilty of murder and the defendant was sentenced to death. The appeal was more or less a formality and was dismissed. No doubt justice was done but he was a most pitiable little man and despite everything, some of the people who had known him felt very sorry for him, as did the prison officers in whose charge he was before and during the trial. They asked me to speak to him because he would not eat, not that he was on hunger-strike but because he said he could not. He promised me that he would try to eat but did not do so and he must have been very weak by the time the end came. It was a sad irony that he should have escaped Nazi ill-treatment only to be hanged for his own deed in the country where he had found sanctuary.

Happily the experience of having my client hanged was not repeated in any subsequent murder case in which I appeared.

Chairman of a Mental Health Review Tribunal

My normal work at the Bar was not my only activity. Although who is and who is not going to get Silk is always supposed to be a closely-guarded secret, before the date when the new Silks were to be announced I had a very good idea that I should succeed. This was because in early March 1960 I was invited to become Chairman of one of the new Mental Health Review Tribunals to be set up under the Mental Health Act of 1959. It seemed to me that this was not an appointment which would be considered suitable for a member of the junior Bar. The country was divided into 15 areas, Birmingham, to which I was appointed, being the largest.

This was a new departure as I had never before been responsible for any organisation. The Chief Regional Officer of the Ministry of Health in Birmingham was Clerk to the Tribunal. He was exceedingly helpful and efficient members of his staff did much of the day-to-day work. I was allotted a room in the Ministry building, with a carpet and two telephones – status symbols I gathered. The Tribunal sat with a minimum of three members, one from each of the three panels, legal, medical and lay. Additional members might sit if the Chairman so desired. A member of the legal panel presided. I did so myself unless I was unavoidably committed elsewhere. In some difficult cases I was glad to have the assistance of two or even three of the consultant psychiatrists who constituted the medical panel. The lay members were responsible people who had rendered public service of one kind or another. In the area there were over 20 hospitals for the mentally ill or handicapped. The Tribunal sat at one or other of these hospitals.

Our task was to hear applications for discharge by patients compulsorily detained or some other person with a qualifying interest, usually a close relative or spouse, on their behalf. The Tribunal could direct discharge or no discharge or alternatively direct reclassification of the patient. In the first year 55 applications were heard. Additionally there were separate meetings of the members of each panel.

Some of the applications were necessarily rather harrowing. Perhaps among the saddest were those of patients incapable of leading an independent life but who nevertheless could have been discharged if there had been members of their families able and willing to care for them.

As Chairman I could, and did, ask to see round some of the hospitals. This provided some interesting experiences; for example walking with the Superintendent round the garden of a hospital for the mentally handicapped when a brick came hurtling over a hedge and narrowly missed us. I took rather a poor view of this, but although the assailant was hidden by the hedge, the Superintendent smiled deprecatingly and said, "Oh, that's George. He does things like that." On another occasion in a ward for mentally ill women I saw what appeared to be a little girl playing with a doll. I took her to be about eight or ten years old but I was told that her age was 26. In a different hospital a ward for mentally ill women looked unusually attractive. The Matron told me that the women there had been a most destructive lot: they had contrived to smash very thick hospital crockery, particularly their tea things and they had repeatedly torn up their bedlinen. Despite criticism that it was folly, the Matron had managed to buy them a pretty tea set of thin china and pretty bedspreads. The destructiveness had stopped immediately and the tea set and bedspreads had become objects of pride and care.

Quite often on my visits I was struck by the understanding and patient care of some of the nurses and the teachers of the subnormal. At one hospital for the mentally handicapped I saw boys and young men who, to the eye of an untrained observer, looked to be incapable of learning or doing anything, yet they were performing quite complicated tasks in a workshop and their pride in displaying their skills was wonderful to behold. Their instructor was obviously a most dedicated and remarkable man for whom one felt a profound admiration.

Commissioner of the Manchester Crown Court

The Mental Health Review Tribunal was not my only activity other than practice at the Bar. I continued to sit at Birmingham Quarter Sessions from time to time for one to three weeks on end according to the pressure of work there. Then in the summer of 1961 I became a Commissioner of the Crown at Manchester, at that time the only Crown Court outside London. Unlike Quarter Sessions the Court had jurisdiction to try all crimes including murder. It was presided over by the full-time Recorder but murder and some other grave offences were in practice tried by a High Court judge sitting at Manchester Assizes who came to the Crown Court for the purpose.

This was the first time a woman had been appointed a Commissioner and there was considerable debate, in which I took no part, as to how I was to be addressed in court. As was the case at the Central Criminal Court, all those who sat at the Manchester Crown Court were addressed as 'My Lord' even though they were not High Court judges for whom (with members of the London Mayor's Court, the Court of Appeal and the House of Lords) this is normally reserved. The decision was reached that 'My Lord' was the only proper form of address, 'My Lady' or 'Madam' being impermissible. So 'My Lord' I became. This caused some amusement to my husband who asked "If she is 'My Lord' what does that make me?" Occasionally the jury looked a little puzzled when counsel used the traditional phrase "My Lord will direct you as to the Law." Perhaps they wondered when His Lordship would condescend to put in an appearance. Equally puzzling must have been my description on the official calendar of prisoners prepared for each Sessions as 'Mr Commissioner, Elizabeth Kathleen Lane, Q.C.'.

One feature which I found interesting when in a northern court for the first time, after experience only in the Midlands and the south, was the different way in which some of the witnesses gave their evidence. As an odd little example of this, in one case when counsel asked the witness if he lived at No 1 High Street, Salford (or wherever) the answer was a loud and emphatic "I do not". Further south it would probably have been something like "Well, I used to but I've moved." Sometimes further south one could sense that although a witness agreed with something put to him by counsel he did not really wish to do so. I never observed this in Manchester: there, any reluctance to agree was likely to be expressed in a phrase such as "That's not right". No doubt these different attitudes of witnesses were well understood by their local juries and by the High Court judges who sat in different places all over the country.

When I first sat in Manchester the Crown Court was held in the rather out-of-date Court House in Minshull Street which the magistrates normally used. In the public gallery there were usually a number of men of the criminal classes, well-accustomed to their surroundings but, temporarily at any rate, out of jail. They took a lively, one might say almost professional, interest in the cases being tried. No doubt they saw some of their friends in the dock from time to time. In one case, after I had passed sentence on a number of men for an attempted bank robbery, my usher went up to the gallery and listened to what was being said. He reported this to me in unvarnished terms: "You've gone wrong this time, the gallery says that so-and-so (the ring leader) should have had 12, not ten, years, and so-and-so should have had seven, not nine years." It was illuminating to have expert opinion of my sentences.

Later on the Court moved to the new Crown Court building, much more imposing and convenient although inevitably with less character of its own. Perhaps the gallery cohort did not feel so much at home there for I do not remember seeing them again after we left Minshull Street.

One case in Manchester which I recall with no pleasure at all was that of a young man against whom there was virtually no evidence except a confession of guilt which he had made and signed at the police station. The jury was sent out of Court while I heard a submission that the confession had not been freely made but induced by the grossly improper behaviour of a police officer in hitting him so hard on the ear that it bled. The defendant was not of good character and I found his evidence quite unconvincing and did not accept it. I saw no reason to doubt the police officer's denial of the assault. The defendant asked if he could call his wife as a witness but when I said that he could, he decided not to do so. I ruled that the confession was admissible in evidence, the jury was recalled and we went through the performance again. But this time the defendant did call his wife: she told how she had seen her husband in the police station, with blood coming from his ear and said that she had roundly abused the police officer for his assault, which he did not deny. She was of somewhat unprepossessing appearance but as I listened to her I became increasingly sure that she was telling the truth. By then it was too late to exclude the statement as it had already been put in evidence before the jury. What I could and did so was to impress upon the jury that if they felt any doubt about the confession having been freely given they must acquit. They did. Whether in fact the defendant was guilty was of much less importance than the necessity for any confession used in evidence to be freely made. It may be that the contents of the statement were true or even that the blow on the ear had been provoked by something said or done by the defendant and not with the intention of making him 'talk', but no matter.

Another case had a very different flavour. A young man had been remanded on bail; he 'jumped' his bail and had to be found, arrested and brought to court for his trial. A friend of his who was serving a sentence was brought from prison as a witness. At the conclusion of his evidence, quite without any prompting, the witness volunteered a statement to this effect: "I told him he was a fool to skip. I said that if he hadn't done what he was charged with he should have gone to Superintendent Haig who was absolutely straight up and would help him and get it sorted out." I was glad that Superintendent Haig was present in Court to hear this. (I hope that I have correctly remembered his name and rank.)

I have a great admiration and respect for the police force of this country which I believe to be the best in the world. Of course there are officers who misbehave; it is almost inconceivable that in a force of such size it could be otherwise. But, at any rate in serious cases, they are usually found out and dealt with appropriately. It must be very frustrating for a police officer to be certain that a suspect is guilty and yet to realise, or be told by a superior, that the evidence is not strong enough to 'make it stick'. I have never known of a policeman who tried to get a man convicted whom he did not believe to be guilty. Police officers are required to work hard, to be courageous and to exercise such self-discipline and restraint as would not readily be found outside the force. It is by this criterion that their conduct is to be judged. A defence of self-defence, or the necessity to use force in the execution of their duty, is open to them but a defence of provocation is not. The question to be asked is not how the ordinary man in the street would react to a given situation but how a trained police officer should, despite being subject to temptations which do not arise for the ordinary man. It is well to keep in mind the debt of gratitude we owe to the police: they are our first line of defence against unlawful conduct including civil disorder and, in the last resort, anarchy.

In the year following my appointment as a Crown Court Commissioner I sat at Manchester for four periods of three to four weeks.

Recorder of Derby

At the end of 1961 I was appointed Recorder of Derby. I was not the first woman to hold such an appointment: Rose Heilbron became Recorder of Burnley in 1956.

A Recordership is an ancient and honourable office. The Lord Mayor or Mayor is always the first citizen of a city or borough, the Recorder the second. Both of them were required to be in attendance upon any visiting Royalty. If one appeared as counsel at the Assizes in the county where one was a Recorder one was not addressed by name by the judge but as 'Mr Recorder'.

Although I was then no longer a Recorder I was very sad when Quarter Sessions were abolished by the Courts Act of 1971. We still have Recorders but they are no longer Recorders of any particular place and sit in a Crown Court here, there and everywhere. Administratively this may be desirable or even necessary but in my view a Recorder who got to know his people, his probation officers and his police, and was known by them, was in an advantageous position to administer justice locally.

Derby may not be one of our most beautiful towns but it is an interesting one with quite an important place in history. Amongst its claims to fame is that football was invented and first played there, also it had the first silk mill in England, five storeys high, built on an island in the River Derwent and still preserved.

The previous Recorder had held office for 28 years and had had the reputation of never sending anyone to prison or, if he did, only for a very short term. Any serious crimes committed in the borough were, if possible, sent for trial at Assizes. Fortunately Derby was a fairly law-abiding community. Partly, I think, this desirable situation was due to the good relationship between police and populace. This relationship was fostered in different ways: for example, at regular intervals police motor-cyclists gave up their free evening time to give instruction in the maintenance and repair of motor cycles. Advantage was taken of this by young men who would attend auction sales at which they could pick up broken-down motor cycles very cheaply, push them, sometimes for many miles, to Derby police station where they were helped to put the machines into safe working order.

Another event which encouraged the relationship was the annual police garden party. There was an open invitation to everyone in the town to attend and many did so. They were regaled with tea and buns and got to know their local officers.

In some cases I was struck by how much help the Derby people gave the police. If an officer was in difficulty he could be pretty sure that people would come to his aid. If there was a noise in the night of breaking glass from a neighbour's house the police would be sent for but men of the neighbourhood might well be prepared to turn out and surround the house even before the police arrived.

There was one particular officer in the force whose brother was a probation officer. Between them they managed to keep a number of youngsters out of trouble.

Perhaps it was not only the very much smaller population which caused the Derby Quarter Sessions Calendars to be so much lighter than those of Manchester and Birmingham. On the four occasions when I sat at Derby the Sessions only lasted for two or three days.

As I was already spending rather more time on other activities than was good for my practice, once I had my own Recordership I ceased to sit at Birmingham Quarter Sessions. One acquires a certain amount of kudos from holding appointments but what solicitors require is that one should be available for court work, not away for substantial periods on other duties. Looking back at my fee book I am surprised that I had so many cases as I did when I was in Silk.

Bar clerks

My clerk was pleased that I had finished with Birmingham. He was always very good about my absences and never complained but it is a real disadvantage to the clerk for his principals to be away from practice. While a barrister is paid (modestly) for sitting as a Commissioner and the like, the clerk receives nothing for this, whereas he is entitled to his clerk's fee on each Bar case. In some instances the senior clerk is paid a fixed minimum salary plus the whole or a proportion of the clerk's fees but in any case he benefits from his principals' Bar earnings. This may also apply to the junior clerk(s). Some clerks earn more than any of their principals; before a barrister has acquired a practice he earns a mere pittance compared with the clerk of busy chambers.

The Bar clerk is unique, there is no other occupation similar to his: he is a loyal servant, a confidant, and in a sense a paymaster. it is his responsibility to ensure that one gets to the right Court at the right time and with the right papers. One should be completely frank with him: if one has offended a solicitor or been scolded by the judge, it is wise to tell the clerk (he would probably hear about it anyway). Equally one may tell him that one has done a case well or been praised by the judge (he is perhaps less likely to hear of this from elsewhere). He is also a protective barrier: solicitors cannot approach counsel except through the clerk. He agrees the fees with the solicitor and it is one of his skills to know how to value the services of each of his principals. Solicitors may ask a clerk to advise on which of the barristers in the

Chambers would be most suitable for a particular case, or the clerk may be handed a brief (not a very important one) and invited to give it to whoever he chooses. This is where a clerk may influence the career of a young barrister by seeing that he gets his fair share of such briefs. A Bar clerk generally makes himself agreeable to solicitors and their clerks, but no touting for briefs is allowed. A clerk identifies himself completely with his principals and may say "I" when he means "He". There is an old chestnut about the Bar clerk saying to a solicitor "Sorry, I can't take that brief for tomorrow. I am on my feet at the Old Bailey doing a murder."

Barristers and solicitors

In the witch-hunt for monopolies it is recurrently argued that there should be fusion of the Bar and solicitors, an argument also put forward by others better qualified to speak than some of the witch-hunters. The examples of the United States and Australia are cited in support. I am unshakeably convinced that such fusion would irreparably damage our administration of justice. A number of barristers work in the same set of Chambers with the same clerk but every one of them is completely independent and there are no partnerships. The strict discipline of the Bar could not be reproduced if there were an amalgamation with the vastly greater number of solicitors, although the latter of course have their own disciplinary system. Judges and others in authority get to know the comparatively few members of the Bar and to know which of them are the most reliable and competent. Barristers are experts in law and advocacy and it would be a great pity on the one hand to deprive them of their independence and turn them into partners responsible to one another and on the other hand to confine them to a particular firm instead of their being available to all solicitors and lay clients. It would be no more sensible to

113

abolish the distinction between barristers and solicitors than it would be in the case of medical consultants and general practitioners.

The Midland Circuit

As a Silk one continues to practice in London and on one's Circuit. The Midland Circuit (it was after my day that it became the Midland and Oxford Circuit) provided a great variety of civil work. Broadly speaking, at Aylesbury, Bedford, Northampton and Lincoln there were a good many agricultural cases, so it was desirable to know or to learn something about farming; at Lincoln there were also cases from Grimsby concerned with the fishing industry which involved trawler accidents; at Leicester, Derby and Nottingham there were coal mine cases as well as many other kinds of industrial cases; at Birmingham there were numerous cases concerning heavy industry so an ability to understand the working or machinery was important; at Warwick there was a mixture of agricultural and industrial cases. Road accident cases appeared everywhere as did many other kinds of action, e g fraud, breach of contract, defamation and so on.

The companionship on the Midland Circuit was, I think, particularly close.

The Circuit had its 'characters' of course. For example there was one successful member of the junior Bar who had great trouble with his S's. Too close companionship with him when he was speaking might have undesirable consequences. Another member of the Circuit, with a reputation for sharp wit, who was once appearing against him took a furled umbrella into court and threatened to put it up if he did not keep his head averted when speaking. The same wit on being told that the other had had a fire in his Chamber remarked "No doubt he extinguished the conflagration with a few well-chosen words."

114

Arthur Ward

Then there was the redoubtable Arthur Ward who took Silk and was successful before and after doing so. He had a way with juries which made him much sought after in some criminal cases. When addressing a jury he had a habit of wagging a forefinger at them and saying "But members of the jury it does not stop there" before going on to his next point. He was a fearsome cross-examiner: I once saw him reduce a police inspector (whom I thought to have given fair and truthful evidence) almost to pulp, his face covered with sweat and contradicting himself several times. Not the sort of cross-examination which some of us would have wished to emulate. He led me once when I was a junior in a civil action concerning a gambling debt. He was a racing man and knew a lot about the tricks of the betting game. The usual practice when a Silk and a junior were briefed was, before the hearing took place, for the junior to prepare a careful note of the facts for the Silk. He might also make notes of the relevant authorities. But the main responsibility for the law rested with the Silk. In this particular case, however, Arthur asked me not to bother with the facts but to leave them to him. What I was to do was to get up the law and bring to court all the relevant authorities together with a note on them. We met at court shortly before the hearing began. I staggered in to see him with an arm-breaking pile of books (I had no clerk with me) and a note on all the cases. He glanced at the note, looked at the pile and said "Dear girl, you have forgotten the most important one." I was taken aback and asked which one. He put his hand in his pocket and produced a copy of *Ruff's Guide to the Turf* – which he placed on top of my pile.

He led me in another civil action, this time for defamation. The slander of which the plaintiff complained was that the defendant had accused him of stealing a horse. The parties were neighbouring farmers. We had one star witness who was to testify to having heard the accusation in the public house where it was alleged to have been made. When we reached court we were dismayed to learn that our witness had either died or gone to Australia, I cannot remember which, but he was certainly not available. This left us with nobody but the plaintiff himself. We knew that the defendant had several witnesses who had been within earshot when the altercation took place in which the words were alleged to have been uttered. They were prepared to say that nothing to that effect had been said. The defendant's advisers would not have known at that stage that we had lost our witness otherwise they might not have accepted a settlement which Arthur proposed to them (I was not present when he did, so I do not know what he said) but a settlement was reached. This was for a statement to be read out in open court to the effect that the defendant did not aver that the plaintiff stole the horse – and regretted if anything he had said had been misunderstood as meaning that the plaintiff was a thief. Each side was to pay its own costs. The plaintiff's costs were quite heavy, our fees alone were substantial. After the case had been called on and disposed of as agreed, our instructing solicitor said that the plaintiff was very upset and wished to see us. He was most disgruntled and said that he did not understand what we had done; that he had been vindicated and yet had to pay his own costs. I remember Arthur's response: "Good gracious man the winning cock expects to lose a few feathers!" This appeared to satisfy him and he had no more to say. Although once instructed, counsel has full responsibility for the conduct of the case it is usual for the lay client to be consulted about a proposed settlement. I suppose that Arthur realised that this plaintiff might not agree to what was proposed and that if he did not he would very probably lose the action and have to pay the defendant's costs as well as his own.

Arthur really loved his work. Once many years ago he was very ill with double pneumonia and other ills. Unexpectedly he recovered. I remember his first appearance in court afterwards; initially I thought that he looked quite unfit for it. At the beginning of the case he could hardly raise his voice above a hoarse whisper but before it finished his voice was as loud and penetrating as ever and his gestures just as energetic. When the case was over I remarked on this to him and asked how it happened. His answer was: "It was the smell of powder to the old war horse." Perhaps I was basely suspicious in wondering whether the early part of his performance had not been something of an act put on to gain sympathy.

He is long dead now and he had no children so I have not hesitated to name him. Perhaps in some circles he did not enjoy the most enviable reputation, but out of court he was a kind and generous man and also very amusing. Advocacy was more of a joy than work to him and I can just picture him at the Pearly Gates arguing with St Peter about the judgment to be given.

Paul Sandlands

Paul Sandlands, to whom I have referred earlier, was something of a 'character' in his own way. He was far from being flamboyant but was quietly and persistently persuasive and a formidable opponent. He led me in a number of cases but happily I never appeared against him. He sometimes seemed to take a gloomy view of his case shortly before it was due to come on which was apt to perturb his instructing solicitors. In one instance when I was his junior a conference took place on the afternoon before the hearing when he seemed to be thoroughly dissatisfied with our case and the likelihood of success. The solicitor said to me afterwards that it was most upsetting to find that, although I had advised that the case had a very good chance of success, the leader appeared to take such a different view. I told him not to worry, that once morning came the leader would be full of confidence. So he was. We won.

Only once did I see Paul lose his temper in court (or out
of it for that matter). He was instructed by a solicitor who
was what we called a 'gown-tugger', one who had that
sometimes maddening habit when counsel was on his
feet of tugging his gown to attract his attention and
whispering some suggestion or information to him.
Occasionally, during a hearing a solicitor has something
important to say, in which case counsel may ask the
judge to allow him a few moments to take further
instructions, which is invariably granted and the trial is
held up while he does so. But this particular solicitor was
really infuriating and should have known better,
especially with an eminent Silk, than to tug his gown
every few minutes in order to say something unhelpful if
not pointless. Finally Paul could bear it no more, picked
up a very heavy book, turned round and hit the solicitor
on the top of the head with it, saying "Now will you be
quiet!" It was of course not a heavy blow, but it worked
and the solicitor did not tug again.

Richard Elwes

Richard Elwes Q.C. afterwards Mr Justice Elwes, was
also a character to remember. He had the reputation of
being the best-looking man at the Bar, had a beautiful
voice (his father was Gervase Elwes, the singer), and a
charm and delicacy of touch which were almost unri-
valled. Incidentally, he wrote very good poetry. I once
listened spell-bound at his skill in a case where he was
defending a man charged with a sexual offence against
quite a small girl. I do not remember how old she was,
but the Judge decided that she was fit to give evidence.
Richard had the unenviable task of cross-examining the
child: it is always a difficult task which must be performed with tact and gentleness. Yet the child must be
questioned to show, if possible, that her complaints are
not correct. As is well known, some little girls (and older

ones) may invent such allegations and some may be put up to doing so by other people. This is why a jury is always warned that it is dangerous to convict unless there is corroborative evidence. If, at the end of a trial the defendant is found guilty he may have made matters worse for himself in the eyes of the judge by causing the child to be subjected to a court appearance and cross-examination. This is also so in cases of sexual assaults on girls and women of any age. It is not that a judge will increase what is the appropriate penalty for the particular offence, but that the defendant may not receive a possible discount for having spared the complainant an unnecessary ordeal.

Rex Vaughan

Richard Elwes died some years ago as did one of the other 'characters', Rex Vaughan Q.C. He became successively Recorder of Lincoln and Recorder of Birmingham. He had a less subtle approach than Richard, more of a head-on attack, and when the two were opposed in court it was like watching a battle between a man armed with a heavy club (Rex) and one armed with a rapier (Richard). The outcome was never a foregone conclusion, it depended ultimately on the strengths of their respective cases, but one could be sure of both sides being well represented.

Rex liked to spend his evenings in conviviality rather than in working, but he woke very early in the ensuing mornings, at 3.00 am if necessary, and worked in bed with his papers strewn over the bedclothes, or so he told me. This sometimes meant that before dawn on the day of the hearing he knew little about his case. Once when he was my leader we had a conference at about 5.00 pm on the eve of the trial and I had to keep on intervening in an endeavour to hide his ignorance of the case. But I did not succeed and the solicitor (who was a regular client of mine but not of Rex's) was somewhat irate and complained to me afterwards that it was obvious that the leader knew next to nothing about the case. I was able to reassure him that before we went into court the leader would have a complete mastery of the case. And so he had. (A junior had other functions besides soothing anxious solicitors!)

There were many other 'characters' on the Circuit, such as Maurice Healy Q.C. but, as this is not meant to be a history of the Circuit, I will cite no more examples.

Even allowing for natural bias in their favour it seems to me that, in general, the Bar comprises some of the most pleasant, kindly, upright and hardworking people I have ever known. Yet oddly they share the mislike and mistrust felt by some of the public for lawyers in general. Hence those opprobrious litle sayings such as:

'The only difference between a barrister and a solicitor is that between an alligator and a crocodile.'

'A lawyer lies first on one side and then on the other and when he is dead he lies still.'

And a particularly nasty dig by Coleridge:

> 'He saw a Lawyer killing a viper
> On a dunghill hard by his own stable,
> And the Devil smiled, for it put him in mind
> Of Cain and his brother Abel.'

This antipathy for lawyers is nothing new, far from it, one of the classical Roman authors (Cicero?) it was who wrote:

> 'Advocatus sed non latro
> Res miranda populo.'

> ('An advocate but not a robber,
> A marvellous thing to the people.'
> – my translation, academic Latinists may quibble).

Never mind, the Bar can take it: they know better.

Anyway in Silk as well as in stuff I was very proud and happy to belong to the profession and when the time came for me to leave it I knew that I should miss the happy life in Chambers and the companionship of other members of the Bar. And I did.

Chapter 9

In the county court

In August 1962 Randall and I were on holiday in Majorca. On an exceedingly hot day we played several strenuous sets of tennis against two Frenchmen. When this was over one of the Frenchmen ran down to the beach, threw his racket down on the sand and plunged into the sea, shoes and all. Randall and I went back to the hotel looking forward to more conventional ablutions. My mind was still full of tennis balls when the hall porter put into my sticky hand a most official-looking letter. It contained an invitation from the Lord Chancellor to accept appointment as a county court judge. If the earth had opened before me I could not have been more astonished. True, years earlier, I had applied to be considered for such appointment but I only did so because of the urging of other women barristers who argued that unless such applications were made it could be said that women did not want to become judges. I had thought that the application was hopeless if not silly.

Applications were required for Silk, customary for Recorderships, permissible for county court judgeships but never allowed for High Court judgeships.

There could be no question of my refusing the invitation even if I had wished to (which was not the case), or my name would have been anathema to every other woman at the Bar.

Fortunately Randall and I were able to finish our month's holiday so there was time to get used to the idea before facing up to the actuality. It was an alarming prospect, not made any less so by the great publicity given to my appointment. I realised that if I made mistakes even such as might not attract attention in the case of a male judge, they certainly would do so in mine and I should be letting down the Lord Chancellor, the late Lord Dilhorne, who had shown such bold originality in appointing a woman, as well as damaging the chances of other women at the Bar. In the event of course I made some mistakes but not of the kind to attract publicity. It is no disgrace for one's decisions to be taken to the Court of Appeal, so far as I know it happens to every judge. I daresay that I am being too kind to myself but I can only remember being reversed in one county court case and in one undefended divorce when I had refused to grant a decree.

In the previous chapter I referred to the way in which Bar clerks were identified with their principals: there was a nice little example of this after my appointment had been announced but before I started to sit, when I was walking through the Temple with my senior clerk and we met the clerk from other Chambers. He gave me a brief greeting and then said to my clerk "Congratulations! You are the only clerk in the Temple who could have done it." I did think that I had had something to do with my appointment myself but no matter.

Circuit 38

To begin with, I was told, I should be a 'floater', that is to say might be required to sit anywhere from Newcastle to Penzance in order to assist or deputise for the local county court judge. But before I took up my appointment I was invited instead to become the second judge on Circuit 38 which comprised Edmonton, the principal court, Watford, Barnet, St Albans and Hertford. I did not learn until later that this had already been offered to other county court judges and declined, perhaps because Circuit 38 had the reputation of being the most overworked Circuit of them all. But this would not have altered my acceptance even if I had known of it. I was never averse to hard work and I was delighted with the prospect of being at home every night and of knowing exactly where I should be every day for up to a year ahead. No longer should I have to try the patience of my long-suffering friends by accepting invitations on terms that I could 'give back word' if I found that I had to be away, or having to restrict my own hospitality to dates when I was reasonably sure that I should be in London. This prospect also appealed to Randall.

His Honour Judge Granville Smith was the senior judge of the Circuit, who showed no resentment at having a woman as number two, on the contrary he was welcoming and kind. Occasionally we both sat at Edmonton on the same day but normally we were at different courts.

The reputation of being a hard-worked Circuit was deserved. I frequently sat until between 5.30 and 6.30 pm and occasionally until later in order to finish the list and save the costs and inconvenience to the parties of having to come back on another day. On the other hand it was seldom necessary to work at home in the evening. Once a month we had a day off, officially known as a 'Judgment Day'. The purpose was to enable one to write any reserved judgments. I think that I am right in saying that I only reserved judgment in two cases so that day was more 'off' than 'judgment', although sometimes it was very useful for reading up one's notes and the documents in a case which had been adjourned and was coming back into the list. Also one was quite often asked to address magistrates, university students and others and could arrange to do so on one's day off.

No problems arose about the way I was to be addressed in court: 'Your Honour' was sexless and 'Her Honour' instead of 'His Honour' was easy.

Although I had appeared in county courts as a member of the junior Bar I had not realised what a lot there was to learn about the procedure and it took some time to become familiar with it. Initially it seemed quite extraordinary that people could sue for, say, £30 and I had to make radical adjustments to my ideas about damages.

The parties were sometimes represented by barristers, more usually by solicitors and quite often not represented at all. With two litigants in person one had to help them both and then judge between them. Without the assistance of counsel or a solicitor one had to rely entirely on one's own knowledge of the law. The Circuit had a library but it was split up between the courts, although the standard textbooks were available in all of them.

One of the most satisfying aspects of the work was being able on occasions to make peace between quarrelling litigants, although the majority of disputes could only result in a finding in favour of one side, to the detriment and sometimes the disgust of the other. But, for example, one could sometimes persuade a landlord to allow a tenant to stay on for a longer period than could be ordered by the court, or get the parties to agree to split the difference in some disputed claim. It was also satisfying to be able at times to protect hire-purchasers from the oppression of some of the hire-purchase financiers. The large and reputable finance companies were usually reasonable enough and allowed their borrowers considerable latitude but there were one or two small ones in the Edmonton area which I was happy to thwart when the occasion arose. I recall a particular case where the defendant hire-purchaser had missed paying one or two instalments owing to some unforeseen circumstance and said that he had written to what was really the one-man business which had financed the transaction explaining what had happened and asking for time to pay. The plaintiff denied having received the letter but there was something about the way in which the defendant had said what he did that made me feel pretty sure that he was speaking the truth. So I took a hand myself and cross-examined the plaintiff as to possible mis-filing, mislaying and so forth. All I received were the most positive assertions that as the letter was not in the file he had brought to court it was impossible that it could have been received. The defendant kept quiet while this was going on and then produced from his pocket a letter from the plaintiff acknowledging receipt of the one in question. The plaintiff received a dressing-down which he was unlikely to forget. I do not think that he appeared before me again.

In another hire-purchase case concerning a car the finance company, again a small one, was run by men who did not appeal to me at all and who had assaulted the hire-purchaser, manhandled him out of the car and re-possessed it when they were not entitled in law to do so. This time the plaintiff was the hire-purchaser suing for damages for the assault and the seizure of the car. I awarded him the highest damages I could and described the company and its officers in terms which I hoped would make them hesitate before doing the same thing again. When I left the court that evening it crossed my mind that someone might be lying in wait for me, but my fears were groundless. Later the company moved out of the area.

Judgment summonses

Judgment summonses occupied a good deal of time, 80 or more in one's list needed to be taken quickly if they were to be finished in the day. Often the same debtor appeared time after time with various creditors. I got tired of this and decided to tackle the problem differently. Not more than 14 to 18 summonses were listed for one day. Then, instead of the usual almost perfunctory procedure, each case was investigated thoroughly and ways explored in which, given time, the judgment debt could be met. This proved to be a saving rather than a waste of

time. Then I devised a scheme whereby all the creditors
of a particular debtor were brought to court together and
the debtor's means to pay carefully investigated. If possible with the agreement of the creditors, a sum was
arrived at representing the maximum the debtor could
reasonably be called on to pay, then came the task of
dividing up the amount between the creditors, the larger
and longer-standing debts having a greater share than the
others. It was striking how reasonable the creditors
usually were and thankful to receive five shillings or even
one shilling a week regularly rather than repeatedly
coming back to court for an order which might not
produce any money. I used to emphasise to the debtor
how adventageous the arrangement was to him and warn
him that if he did not keep up the payments he would be
in danger of an order committing him to prison. This
was not a formal administration order but I believe that
subsequently the procedure was adopted on a more formal basis than my own.

No doubt when the law was amended to allow
betting-shops this got rid of a good many irregularities
and abuses but I did not welcome it. On a number of
occasions a man who had received a summons for possession of his house on the ground of non-payment of
rent satisfied me that he had given the rent money
regularly each week to his wife who had confessed to
having lost it in a betting-shop. Perhaps the novelty of
the temptation has worn off by now.

Not infrequently a debtor disappeared and could not
be traced. I was sitting at Watford one day when there
was a great rumpus in the hall, the court door was flung
open and in came three or four men holding on to
another. The other was a missing debtor who owed a lot
of money on a judgment debt to a farmer. Summons
after summons had been issued but never served because
he could not be found. That morning the debtor had been
foolish enough to reappear and walk across the farmer's
land where he was spotted by some of the farm labourers

who knew all about the debt. They had grabbed him and brought him forcibly to court, a considerable distance away. I was not at all sure that they were within the law in doing so but never mind, there he was and it was at last possible to deal with him appropriately.

Some landlords and tenants

Sometimes a tenant appeared complaining of harrassment or unlawful eviction, or both, by a landlord. Less often a landlord was faced with untrue accusations of the same kind. There were some pretty tough characters in the Edmonton district and it was not always easy to determine where the truth lay. The question why had they not complained to the police of being assaulted met with the stock answer, which might or might not be true, that fear of the landlord and his bullyboys had deterred them from doing so. Some landlords, particularly women, put up with appalling behaviour for a long time before daring to bring court proceedings because of threats by their tenants.

Adoptions

A very different class of case heard in the county court was that of adoption applications. These were heard in Chambers and treated confidentially so I am not at liberty to refer to any particular one of them. It was very satisfying to order that a child who would otherwise have led a miserable life, or at best been brought up in an institution, should be adopted by people who would provide a stable and happy home and real affection. On the other hand it was heartrending if a parent, usually unmarried, withdrew consent at the last minute when the would-be adopters and the child had grown attached to each other during the compulsory pre-adoption period together.

Since my day the law has grown more liberal about dispensing with parental consent in such cases and, however strongly one may uphold the rights and responsibilities of parents, I am sure that the change is right.

Divorce

At the Bar I had never been concerned with adoption cases but I was familiar with divorce cases so it was less strange to sit for one day a fortnight as a Special Commissioner of Divorce in the High Court. In those days county courts had no jurisdiction in divorce and county court judges sitting as Commissioners heard only undefended petitions. Once more the problem arose of a separate robing-room for my use. The solution was found in a curious room in the Law Courts which appeared to be otherwise unused and in which almost the only piece of furniture was, most inappropriately, a grand piano. I was unable to ascertain why it was there or how it ever got there. I resisted the obvious temptation.

London Sessions

In 1965 new legislation came into force which provided for county court judges to sit periodically in criminal courts. One could refuse to do so and some judges did refuse, for instance if they had been Chancery Division practitioners at the Bar and had never been in a criminal court in their lives. A few of the provincial county court judges used to sit as Chairmen of their local Quarter Sessions but none of the London judges did so far as I know. I would dearly have liked to refuse, but clearly I was well experienced in presiding in criminal courts and if I had refused it would have entailed other judges, who might be as reluctant as I was, having to sit for longer

129

periods. But I did refuse to sit for two months on end annually which was to be the allotted stint: I was not prepared to abandon my county courts for so long at a time and I compromised by agreeing to sit for one month twice a year. So in May of that year I sat for four weeks at the London Sessions at Newington Causeway. I disliked it intensely: the whole atmosphere was different from the provincial criminal courts I had known. I did not care for some of the court officials; I had some juries which acquitted when the prosecution evidence was overwhelming and there ought to have been convictions, as they must have known. Also the conduct of one or two of the counsel who appeared before me met with my disapproval. As I have said earlier, all this changed and London Sessions deservedly enjoyed a better reputation before being abolished in 1971.

Changes

Since the Courts Act of 1971 came into operation there are no more county court judges: they have become Circuit judges and although they continue to sit in county courts they spend much of their time on criminal work in Crown Courts. No doubt this, like the change in the status and work of Recorders, may be very convenient administratively, but I think that it represents a real loss to the county court. A county court judge sitting constantly learned what the local problems were; he got to know the solicitors practising in his court, which of them were able and helpful and which were less so; he got to know which of the enquiry agents in debt cases were trustworthy and which were less so. All this I found of real assistance in the kind of cases heard in a county court. On the other side of the coin, solicitors and the public generally got to know their local judge and how he ran his court. Geoffrey Howard used to say that if anyone wanted to know what the local county court judge was like the way to learn was by listening to what was said about him in the local public houses.

It is probably true that the local judge used to be a greater power in the land than he was even in my day. Some of the judges were apt to be rather eccentric. There was one who never paid his bills on time: creditors knew what to do, they sued him in his own court. When the cases were called on the Judge would look round the court and say "No appearance by the defendant. Judgment for the plaintiff with costs." Counsel in a north country county court was in the middle of a speech when the Judge rose abruptly and went into his room which opened off the bench, leaving the door open, and called out "Continue with what you were saying, I can hear you from where I am". Then clouds of tobacco smoke were wafted through the doorway into the court. In a case in a London county court where both parties were appearing in person, the defendant repeatedly interrupted the plaintiff in his evidence and was asked by the Judge "Can't you wait until he has finished committing perjury before you do the same yourself?" In another court both litigants were women and while they were in their respective witness-boxes one of them pulled a dead cat out of her bag and flung it across the court at the other one. Said the Judge "Madam if you do that again I shall have to ask you to leave the Court."

Mine were perhaps less colourful days but I found life in the county court happy and rewarding.

Chapter 10
In the High Court and a Bencher

On a county court 'Judgment Day' (day off) late in July 1965 I went out in the morning and bought myself a new hat. When I came home for lunch my housekeeper said that there had been a telephone call for me, which she had not written down, and she could not remember the name of the caller except that it was "something like water and sounded chilly". Not for nothing had I been doing *The Times* crossword puzzle for years and I immediately asked if it was Sir George Coldstream (then the Sectretary to the Lord Chancellor); it was. The message was that I was to go to the House of Lords at 2 o'clock that afternoon as the Lord Chancellor (then Lord Gardiner) wished to see me. My heart nearly stopped beating; what could I have done in the county court which could possibly merit a rebuke from the Lord Chancellor himself? Well, perhaps I had been a bit too sharp with that solicitor and an order I had made was perhaps somewhat unorthodox, but I was sure that I had done nothing which would deserve dismissal. I did not enjoy my lunch, but I put on my new hat and duly presented myself. Sir George, who was the most delightful man and whom I already knew, received me most amiably: he asked me how things were going in the county court, how I was enjoying my life there and so on. This did not sound like trouble ahead but I was mystified. After a few minutes, in which I had not been given the slightest hint of what was to come, I was shown in to the Lord

Chancellor. He was very agreeable and then said that he wished to appoint me a High Court judge assigned to the Probate, Divorce and Admiralty Division. I was stunned, so much so that, to my shame, I had to ask him to repeat what he had said. So that was that.

Randall's comment which, much to my disapproval, he later made to the Lord Chancellor was "I always knew this would happen" – which was a lot more than I did.

People were always very kind in writing letters of congratulation each time I had received an appointment and this time there were more letters than ever, including some from complete strangers, more than one of whom were patients in mental hospitals. One of the latter wrote that she was sorry to see from the newspapers that as the junior judge I should have to walk at the tail end of the Lord Chancellor's procession "but never mind, it's the end of the tail that keeps the flies off."

There was time to order the new robes and then Randall and I went on holiday to Tunisia. I took the letters with me so that I could write my thanks at leisure. The hotel ran out of stamps, so did the local post office (or tobacconist) and I had to wait for more to be procured. Meanwhile the hall porter had become suspicious: no tourist ever wrote so many letters from Tunisia so he concluded that I must be running some sort of racket by post and informed the local police. Randall had a few words with the police (rude ones I daresay) and all was well.

Near disaster

But all was far from well shortly afterwards when we were staying in Hammamet, I fell ill, very ill. Through the British Embassy in Tunis Randall arranged for me to go into hospital there. The surgeon, who I think was French, diagnosed appendicitis, which it was not. The Arab physician disagreed but gave way to the surgeon.

Then a young Arab came into my room, he looked to be about 15 or 16, wore a grubby-looking fez and a very dirty white overall. After some difficulty I made out that he was the anaesthetist. It seemed to me to be extremely unlikely that I should survive and Randall died a thousand deaths. After the operation I ran a high fever and the antibiotics (which were probably leftovers from the army during the last war) were ineffective. Randall got me onto a plane to Rome and thence to London, where my doctor had arranged for an abdominal surgeon and a gynaecologist to attend me. Neither of them could, or ever did, make a certain diagnosis of what had been the matter with me, except that it had not been appendicitis. I was taken to a nursing home, still very ill. By then it was 14 September but I was absolutely determined to recover in time to be sworn in by the Lord Chancellor on the 30th and to attend the annual legal service, followed by the procession to the House of Lords for the 'Lord Chancellor's Breakfast' on 1 October. I just managed it. One of the surgeons said that he had never known a patient fight so hard to recover. I had to; it would have been too awful to start one's High Court career as an absentee and to disappoint the people who expected to see me in the procession (at the tail end). Wearing heavy full robes it was somewhat exhausting but fortunately 1 October was a Friday and I had a couple of days in which to rest before taking my seat on the following Monday.

My clerk

A day or so after my appointment had first been announced Lord Denning telephoned to ask if I had thought of having a woman as judge's clerk. I said that I was still in a state of shock and had not thought about anything. He told me that he had a most excellent secretary who would very much like to be my clerk and asked if I would see her. Within moments of doing so I decided that I could ask for nobody better. Her name was Molly Hall, a widow with grown-up children. She was a remarkable woman, tall, good-looking, sweet tempered, tactful, resourceful, extremely loyal, conscientious, and a beautiful typist. She also played tennis, table tennis and croquet, so if we were on circuit where these facilities were available I was never short of a partner or opponent. She became very popular with everyone who came in contact with her. She was the first woman judge's clerk, so we were beginners together. While I was still a judge a certain aloofness had to be maintained but after we had both retired she came to stay with me once or twice and we played scrabble for hours on end. To my great sorrow she has since died. I am grateful to be able to pay this little tribute to her. I am sure that any of the judges, their clerks, barristers, their clerks, solicitors and court officials who knew her and may read this will be very pleased that it has been done.

D.B.E.

All male High Court judges are knighted by Her Majesty the Queen. Clearly this could not happen to me so Her Majesty created me a Dame Commander of the Order of the British Empire (D.B.E.). According to the table of precedence, a Dame has precedence over a Knight. Not that this made any difference to my position in legal processions and the like: there of course I took my place according to judicial seniority. Like all High Court judges on receiving their honour, I had the great privilege of spending 20 minutes alone with Her Majesty in a drawing-room at Buckingham Palace, during which she presented me with the insignia of a Dame. All that the men receive is the Knight's badge of crossed swords, which, by tradition is never worn, but I was able on suitable occasions to wear the badge of the Order and the silver star. Randall had already been made a Commander of the same Order (C.B.E.) in recognition of his service with the British Council, so we made a nice pair.

On my appointment, inevitably the question arose as to how I should be addressed in court. Was it to be the only known form in the High Court of 'My Lord' or was reality to be faced and was it to be 'My Lady'? This was a matter of discussion in high places and, as I knew what powerful voices were being raised in support of the latter, I deemed it prudent not to put in my oar. All was well and I became 'My Lady'.

Of course it took some time for barristers to grow used to the novelty and for the first few months it was quite often "My Lord, I beg your pardon, My Lady". Early on I had a long case in which Silks were appearing and before it ended they were well accustomed to 'My Lady'. So much so that when one of them went on to his next case which was before one of our more outspoken judges and called him 'Your Ladyship' I was told that the ceiling was almost cracked by the resulting explosion.

A Bencher

High Court judges who are not already Benchers of their Inns of Court are invited on appointment to become such. The Bench is the governing body of an Inn, presided over by the Treasurer of the year, and having a number of Committees such as the Church Committee, the Scholarship Committee and so on. It is a considerable honour to be elected a Bencher.

No woman had ever been a Bencher of an Inn until I came along and invaded this masculine preserve. Other Inns beside the Inner Temple now have women Benchers and my Inn has another two besides myself. I was mostly kindly received and never made to feel the odd one out. Being a Bencher has been a source of great happiness and pride to me.

Once or twice a year the Inn has a 'Grand Day' dinner

to which distinguished guests are invited and evening dress and decorations are worn. When Her Majesty the Queen graciously came to dine with us it was useful to have a woman Bencher and I acted as 'lady in waiting extra-ordinary' as I was referred to by some of my brother Benchers. As such, I was privileged to be in the entrance hall with the Treasurer and the under-Treasurer to receive Her Majesty and conduct her to the Powder Room to leave her wrap.

We took dessert in the library on an upper floor. Thereafter on departure Her Majesty was to come down by the lift. My function was to be there to receive her when she left the lift. I could not travel in the lift but had to use the staircase. Of course nobody could rise from the table before her so I had to wait until she did so and then make a dash for the stairs. I gathered up my long dress and came down the two flights faster, I am certain, than anyone else has ever done. I need not have worried: the royal progress to the lift (perhaps designedly) had been slow and I was there well before the lift arrived. I had time to pop into the Powder Room to make sure that all was well and horrors! the beautiful white ermine wrap had gone. I was aghast, shot out of the room, saw a man in the hall who was obviously a royal detective (he had to be, no other strange man could have been there) and who said that the wrap had already been taken out to the car on the Queen's instructions. My immense sigh of relief almost blew him over.

The same duties were mine when a royal princess came to dine and also when Mrs Thatcher was our guest, but on those occasions dessert was not taken in the library.

Indoor plants

Like all High Court judges, I had my own room in the Law Courts. At first I had a pleasant enough room but later I moved into a much larger one with handsome oak panelling. Between the two parts of the double glazing of the window there was room to grow plants. With a hot pipe running along the floor and the sun shining on the south-facing window it made the best greenhouse I had ever had.

Probate, Divorce and Admiralty

It was the Judicature Act of 1875 which established the three Divisions of the High Court of Justice: Chancery, Queen's (or King's according to which sovereign reigns) Bench, and Probate, Divorce and Admiralty. Probate and Divorce had been within the jurisdiction of the Ecclesiastical Courts set up by William the Conquerer until, by an Act of 1857, they were transferred to the civil jurisdiction and for a brief spell of 18 years each had a separate High Court of their own.

There had been a succession of Maritime and Admiralty Courts before a High Court of Admiralty was established in about 1340. One or two small and ancient Admiralty Courts continued to exist and I believe still do, in theory at any rate, such as that of the Admiral of the Cinque Ports. It has been said that the reason why Admiralty was combined with Probate and Divorce, even though they made rather strange bed-fellows, was that it could not be fitted into either of the other two Divisions. The marriage of Probate, Divorce and Admiralty in one Division endured until they were divorced by the Administration of Justice Act 1971.

(This brief outline omits any reference to many matters important to lawyers but which seem to me to be of less general interest.)

The Administration of Justice Act of 1971 brought substantial changes: the Probate, Divorce and Admiralty Division was re-named the Family Division, contentious Probate cases were transferred to the Chancery Division and Admiralty became a branch of the Queen's Bench Division.

There had been some anomalies before the change: while the Probate, Divorce and Admiralty Division dealt with proof of wills, their construction and administration belonged to the Chancery Division (non-contentious Probate remained in the Family Division for administrative reasons but is dealt with in the Registry). Further, while the Probate, Divorce and Admiralty Division had jurisdiction over children whose parents had resorted to the Divorce Court, wardship, guardianship and High Court adoptions were the province of the Chancery Division. All these were transferred to the Family Division.

The majority, at any rate, of the Family Division judges welcomed the change with respect to children: it was good to have them all under our wing. Speaking personally, I mourned the loss of contested probate actions, which I found very interesting. As to Admiralty cases, these were normally tried in the Probate, Divorce and Admiralty Division by judges who were expert in this branch of the law, having practised in it when at the Bar. I only took one Admiralty case and that was when I was Vacation Judge in August 1970. The owners of a ship named the *Monte Ulia* had a very substantial claim against the owners of a ship called the *Banco*. To call the parties by the names of their ships, the *Monte Ulia* arrested not only the *Banco* but her six sister ships as well. (An Admiralty arrest is usually effected by the Admiralty Marshal affixing the warrant to the mast or other prominent part of the ship for a short while and leaving a copy. Thereafter to move a ship from where she is lying is contempt of court.) The *Monte Ulia* claimed that she was within her rights in so doing by virtue of a section of the Administration of Justice Act 1956: the *Banco* protested that the Act gave no right to arrest more than one ship. This was the point at issue, which had never been previously decided. I should have preferred to reserve my decision at least overnight, so as to have more time to ponder the matter, but it was essential that my decision should be given that day because some of the *Banco*'s sister ships were due to sail that night or the following day. I held that only one ship could be arrested. The *Monte Ulia* appealed to the Court of Appeal but unsuccessfully, so the position in law remains the same.

As to contested probate actions, it seemed to me that litigants were often different from those in any other class of action. For example, the four middle-aged or elderly brothers who lived together in the same house, one of whom had been married, the others were bachelors. One of them decided that they all ought to make mutual wills; this led to fierce quarrels in a normally peaceable household. The one was accused of being morbid and told that it was unlucky to make one's will and so forth. In the end, the one consulted a solicitor who drew up his will and after a while the other three followed suit. Yet when one of them died his will was disputed. In another case an old lady frequently made herself a new will but she never destroyed an old one. She left instructions that her executors would find her will in a piece of furniture with a piece of food upon it. There were many pieces of furniture in the house and after the old lady died the executors found pieces of stale cake, orange peel and the like on a number of chests of drawers and cupboards, each containing an undated will. Cases in which it was alleged that a testator had been of unsound mind or subject to undue influence sometimes revealed people at their grasping worst. In some other cases a testator's spitefulness or ingratitude were equally unedifying, but nevertheless interesting.

In 1971 the Divorce Reform Act of 1969 came into force and radically altered the basis of divorce. The single ground was to be that the marriage had irretrievably broken down but a finding of irretrievable breakdown could not be made unless the Court were satisfied that the respondent spouse had committed adultery and that the petitioner found it intolerable to live with him, or had behaved in such a way that the petitioner could not reasonably be expected to live with him, or had deserted the petitioner for at least two years. Then came an entirely new concept: irretrievable breakdown could also be found if the parties had lived apart continuously for two years and the respondent consented to a divorce, as it could if they had lived apart continuously for five years, whether the respondent consented or not.

(The Act and those which replaced it made many other changes which need not be mentioned here.)

Gone were days of defended petitions on the ground of cruelty which sometimes lasted for days or weeks on end. Speaking personally I rejoiced at their demise. Trying perhaps 30 or even 50 or more separate allegations of cruelty, often of a trivial nature, made by each party, was hardly exhilarating and might involve delving into the secrets of a marriage which would have been better left undisclosed, at any rate in open court.

It was particularly sad when a marriage broke down, from whatever cause, after it had seemingly been success-ful for many years and the parties were of an age when not only their children but perhaps their grandchildren were grown-up.

Children

Saddest of all were the far too frequent cases where there were children who were not grown-up. Sometimes I used to marvel at the blind selfishness of a parent who went off with somebody else or ill-treated the other parent to the knowledge of the children. Yet it often seemed to me that children were happier with two parents who quarrelled than when deprived of one of them, although obviously quarrelling or violence might reach such a pitch that it was better for the children if their parents did part. Perhaps the worst parents of all were those who deliberately set the children against the other parent, or used them as a bargaining counter in financial arrangements.

Of all the heavy responsibilities which any judge has to bear it seems to me that making decisions as to the future of children is the heaviest. With which parent they are to live, how much they are to see of the other, where they are to go to school (if this is in dispute) and so forth will obviously affect their whole lives thereafter. I remember a very experienced judge of my Division saying to me "There never is a right solution of the problem of the children of a broken marriage. All you can do is try to find the lesser of the two evils."

Judges differed in their practice as to seeing children privately when there was a dispute about them. I usually saw them. The welfare officer's report was generally most helpful and often recounted what children had said as to with which parent they wished to live. I never asked that question directly, although sometimes children would volunteer their preference or even beg to be with one parent or the other. Not all the reasons given for the preference were very compelling.

One small boy who was considerably younger than the age at which I normally saw a child, as soon as he came into the room repeated exactly the quite lengthy phrase he had used to the welfare officer as to where he wanted to live. I asked him if he could 'say his tables' and in exactly the same parrot fashion he repeated twice one are two and so on. All the rest of what he said was in a different voice and obviously spontaneous. So I knew what significance to attach to the expressed preference. Apart from a child's preference, what I wanted to ascertain was the kind of child with whom I was concerned and conversation about, for instance, school, pets, football or aeroplanes were often very revealing. Inevitably some of the children tended to be shy but not all of them; one boy of about 12 looked round the bookshelves of law reports lining the walls of my room and said "Cor, you ain't read all them 'ave yer?" And a self-possessed young lady of about ten or eleven who said "Aren't barristers handsome! I'll marry one when I grow up."

I used to be uneasy about the comparatively few children who seemed to be wholly unperturbed by the breakdown of their parents' marriage: those whose school reports showed no signs of disturbance in their work or play and who betrayed no distress to anyone. I used to wonder how much this was due to a genuine lack of feeling about the breakdown and how much to a conscious or unconscious bottling up of feeling which might lead to emotional troubles later on.

Financial arrangements after a divorce occupied a good deal of the judges' time. Frequently it was a question of how far the available means could be stretched to support two homes instead of one. Occasionally one might be concerned with large fortunes perhaps running into millions where, whatever order was made, both parties were going to be much richer than most people can ever hope to be.

On circuit again

Interesting as I found the work of my Division, I was happy to spend part of my time on circuit dealing with the kind of cases I had been concerned with at the Bar, such as negligence, defamation, boundary disputes and contracts.

On circuit, judges live in the Judges' Lodgings which are comfortable and well-staffed domestically. Almost all the Lodgings now are run by the Department of the Environment but in my early days when they were provided by a local council they varied considerably in comfort and staffing and one or two of them left a good deal to be desired.

Judges on circuit are always very kindly entertained by the High Sheriff and others. This hospitality is returned and I found it delightful to be able to say that there would be a dozen or so guests for dinner on a certain date and then to have no responsibility beyond approving or amending the cook's suggested menu, everything else being done by the staff.

Judges on circuit were supposed not merely to represent but actually to be the Sovereign in the county in which they were – unless the Sovereign happened to be in the same county at the same time. On an occasion in Victorian times a junior judge stood up when the loyal toast was proposed after a dinner which the judges were attending, but the senior judge pulled him back into his chair saying, "Sit down you fool, we *are* the Queen." This supposition disappeared during my time but sufficient of it remains to oblige those who entertain the judges to ensure that all other guests arrive before they do and do not leave before them.

When I was appointed it was usual for three or four judges (two or three from the Queen's Bench and one from my Division) to be on circuit together. This made a happy little houseparty, especially if, from time to time a judge's wife or in my case, husband, joined us. After the reorganisation of the circuit work following the Courts Act of 1971 there were often only two judges sitting, or sometimes one alone, but the sittings lasted longer, usually with one or more changes of judge during the same term.

In each of the Lodgings there was a 'Judges' Book' in which the judges recorded their comments on their stay to be read by those responsible for running the Lodgings. These were preserved and could be read by judges in later days. I remember particularly a couple of nineteenth century entries: "Is it not time that one of the modern water closets was installed?" and subsequently "Something should be done about the excessive noise caused when the lavatory pan is flushed." And considerably later on "We wish to have modern horsehair mattresses instead of feather beds."

In the old days judges 'going circuit' travelled in the circuit coach, escorted by pikemen to fend off highwaymen and other miscreants. When a county boundary was to be crossed the coach halted while fresh pikemen from the next county took over from those of the last county.

In modern times judges travel by train and nowadays more often by car. When I first became a judge train travel may have been less fast than it is today, but it was more dignified than it became before I retired. Traditionally, the station master wearing his top hat met the judge on his arrival, or at a London terminus, an assistant station-master wearing a bowler might do so. Judges used to travel with large locked hampers containing their books and other paraphernalia. In those days there were porters at railway stations. Not very long after my appointment hampers were replaced by a large number of suit-cases and holdalls. Mine, together with the clerk's, usually numbered 13. Judges always had a reserved compartment and only their clerks and marshals travelled with them. This not only made for comfort but was also a practical measure to ensure that no litigants or witnesses who were to appear before the judges in court could travel with them. On an occasion during the last war when trains were very crowded, a young army officer was standing in the corridor outside the reserved compartment and could see that there were two or three empty seats in it. After a while he opened the door of the compartment and demanded to know why he could not occupy one of the seats. It was pointed out that the whole compartment was reserved so he went back to the corridor. But a little latter he flung open the door and sat down in one of the seats. The judge gave a nod to his marshal who asked the officer to have a word with him in the corridor. When the situation was made plain the officer went very white and said "My God! I am appearing before him tomorrow charged with motor manslaughter."

When trains ceased to have compartments the best that could be done was to reserve six seats in one of the new coaches. Not so good.

With the same precaution in mind, traditionally judges do not go into hotels or restaurants (except to a function in a private room) in the county in which they are sitting.

In a previous paragraph I referred to a judge's marshal. He is nearly always a budding lawyer and sits on the Bench beside his judge. He goes everywhere with his judge and has to be included in all invitations. He acts as social secretary, writes and acknowledges invitations, pours out the after dinner coffee and makes himself generally useful. It is a great privilege to be a marshal and also highly instructive. Accommodation is provided for him in the Lodgings; years ago it also had to be for the marshal's manservant. Separate accommodation is also provided in the Lodgings for the judge's clerks.

When I was at the Bar it never entered my head that I could be a judge's marshal because all the judges were men. One bold female who asked why she could not be a marshal was firmly told that it was impossible because if judges were unmarried they would feel that they might be compromised and if they were married their wives would not allow it. But when I became a judge I took only women marshals: there were plenty of male judges to take male marshals. After a while the taboo against females melted away and first a judge took his niece and later others took unrelated females. Three of my former marshals still remain good friends of mine.

During my time, most of the judges of my Division spent approximately half of each term sitting in London and the other half on circuit doing the normal work of the Division and also trying criminal cases and civil actions. Criminal prosecutions were given priority over civil actions with the result that, at any rate before the Courts Act of 1971, the latter were subject to long delays and quite frequently sent over to the next Assizes (as the sittings were then called) which might happen more than once. I rebelled against this and insisted that I would attend first to the injured and the widows who, in my eyes, better deserved to have their cases taken than did most of the criminals. If I finished my civil list while there were still crimes to be tried, I was ready to lend a hand, but I think that this only happened twice in the six years before the work of the courts was reorganised so as to minimise the delays.

One of the earliest cases I tried on Circuit was that of an accident in a Derbyshire coal mine in which a miner had been injured. There they all were in court, the solicitor who had always instructed me in such cases when I was at the Bar, the expert whom we had always consulted, the miners' branch secretary and other familiar faces from the past. All of them looking up eagerly at what, I hope, was my impassive face and probably thinking that they were on a good wicket. Alas! I had to find that the case for the plaintiff had not been proved and give judgment for the National Coal Board. I expect that, apart from the solicitor, they regarded me as a traitor.

On my old Bar Circuit it was known that I was familiar with coal-mine accidents, but this was not so elsewhere. When, as a judge, I sat in other coal-mining areas such as Yorkshire or South Wales I used to have a bit of private fun in the first mine accident case I tried there. A look of horror was apt to appear on the faces of the miners when they realised that a woman judge was going to try the case. I used to keep very quiet to begin with and await the right moment to question why something of a very technical nature had not been done, or in a roof-fall case ask to see the Support Rules for the particular mine. The fun came from observing the changing expressions on the faces in court. Unfortunately I could never play the same game twice in the same area because word went round and I was 'rumbled'.

Two of the most indignant litigants I ever came across were plaintiff and defendant in a car collision accident. One was a driving instructor and the other a headmaster, both with long 'clean' driving records. To both of them the allegations of negligent driving was grossly insulting. They gave widely differing accounts of the accident, which, I am sure, each of them believed to be true. When I found them both to blame it was obvious that each of them felt that he had suffered grave injustice. In my experience there was no other class of case in which the parties and perfectly honest independent witnesses gave such irreconcilable accounts of the same event. Quite often one derived more assistance from the damage to the cars involved and to police evidence of measurements, marks or débris on the road and so on, but care was needed here because sometimes the seemingly obvious inference to be drawn from such evidence was not necessarily the right one.

Medical negligence cases were of particular interest to me. Not infrequently consultants disagreed and the judge had to decide between them. In one spinal injury case x-ray photographs were produced at which I was asked to look: the specialists were agreed that I should do so and the first of the consultants assured me that one did not need to be expert in reading x-rays to see plainly that there was damage to certain vertebrae; the other said that what was shown was nothing of the kind but an abnormality which could not have been of traumatic origin. At that moment the lights failed and the windowless court was plunged into darkness. Before I left the court by the light of a police officer's lamp I said that it would be desirable that the two consultants should avail themselves of the unexpected adjournment to discuss the matter and try to reach agreement. When the lights came on again they had done so.

In another back injury case there was no dispute between the consultants that the plaintiff was severely crippled: the most he could do was to walk a few painful yards with the aid of two sticks. For some reason the defendant's insurers became suspicious and engaged a private detective to watch him, with rewarding results. He observed the plaintiff doing repairs underneath his lorry and hurrying up the steps to the top deck of a bus. Finally, from behind some bushes, the detective photographed him breaking in a young horse at the end of a lunging rein. Not a difficult case to decide.

Fraud and malingering in accident cases are not always easy to detect and in some cases I used to think that over-sympathetic medical care aggravated a man's symptoms. On the other hand an over-robust attitude could have the same effect and I sometimes felt sorry for doctors' difficulties in trying to find the right approach.

A plaintiff's anxiety about the outcome of the action and the amount of damages to be recovered can affect some of them severely and the end of the action, even if disappointing, often has a powerfully therapeutic effect.

It is to be hoped that this was so with a plaintiff who bumped his head on a stone arch under which he had to pass at his place or work. The arch was high enough for most men to pass under but he was very tall and failed to duck his head. The result of the bump was what, as children, we called 'an egg' – that is to say a swelling on the forehead in the shape of half an egg. He was not stunned by the impact, there was no damage to his skull and after a few days the 'egg' subsided. A psychiatrist was called as a witness to support his claim that as a result of the accident he was, and would continue to be, incapable of work. Unusually, I attached little weight to the psychiatrist's evidence. He assured me that any injury, however slight, might produce the same psychosomatic effect. I asked whether a small cut on a little finger would suffice and the answer was that it could, to which I said, perhaps improperly, "Not in my Court". I awarded the plaintiff £25 damages. There was no appeal.

In complete contrast was the case of the foundryman who, through someone else's error, had been caught up and crushed in a piece of moving machinery. Both his legs had been amputated above the knee, his ribs had been broken and there were other serious injuries as well. I had read the pleadings before going into court and done a little provisional arithmetic. He was, I think, in his forties and it seemed all too obvious that he would never work again, so it was a matter of so much for lost wages, multiplied by so many years, plus compensation for pain, suffering and loss of amenity. He was brought into court sitting in a wheel-chair and asked me to excuse his coming to court without his artificial legs, explaining that it was going to be a long day for him and he found that wearing the legs for too long at a time became painful. He was back at work, not on the foundry floor but as a storeman at a good wage. His courage, resilience and cheerful determination were unique in my experience in court. I could not award nearly as much for loss of wages as I had expected to do and it would have been wrong in principle to increase the amount as a reward for his heroism, but I do not think that my award was ungenerous.

The Bench is a good place for seeing life, quite frequently at its worst but sometimes at its best.

The Abortion Act Report

In common with a number of other judges, my work was not exclusively confined to judicial duties. In February 1971 I was sitting at Manchester when there was a telephone call asking if I would see an officer from the London Headquarters of the Department of Health and Social Services. I twigged that some kind of enquiry was in the offing. I saw the officer and later when I had returned to London I had an interview with Sir Keith Joseph who was then the Secretary of State for that department. The upshot was that I agreed to chair a Committee to review the working of the Abortion Act 1967. In June 1971 a Committee of 14 other members was appointed, which included two eminent consultant gynaecologists, a professor of psychiatry, two general medical practitioners, other members of the medical and nursing professions, the headmistress of a girls' school and a social worker. And as the Act also applied to

Scotland, a Scottish Q.C. We had a secretary and a medical secretary from the Department staff.

I could not have asked for better Committee members or more efficient secretarial assistance. The members had wide experience of the various ways in which the Act worked and affected women and girls who underwent, or failed to obtain, an abortion and of others including doctors and nurses who were affected by the provisions of the Act and its Regulations.

My own relevant experience was confined to criminal cases of illegal abortion and the appalling consequences which so often ensued. Initially my attitude was more anti- than pro-abortion but the more I learned about it and the better I came to know people who supported legal abortion, the more firmly I came to believe in the rightness of the Act, despite the abuses of it which existed. On the other hand I was wholly unimpressed by those who, sometimes fiercely, advocated abortion on demand and declared that a woman's body was her own and that she was entitled to rid herself of any unwanted object within it.

We held the first of the 33 meetings in June 1971. Sub-Committees which were set up met additionally on 31 days altogether, visited places such as nursing-homes and reported in writing to the full Committee. The full meetings lasted for one, two, three or four days. We met in Oxford for three days and in Edinburgh for two days. The last meeting took place in November 1973 when we submitted our Report to the Secretaries of State for England, for Scotland and for Wales.

We received memoranda or letters from 194 organisations and 529 individuals. (One letter sent to me personally at the Law Courts was addressed to "Naughty Mrs Justice Lane". It read: "I have followed your career with interest for years but I am disgusted with you now you have gone to work for adulterers." Oh dear!) We heard oral evidence from many of these. We sent questionnaires to the NHS hospitals and to nursing-homes approved for abortions and to referral agencies; the Institute for Social Studies in Medical Care carried out a survey for us; the Home Office made a survey for us of foreign women coming to London; all Chief Police Officers in England and Wales were asked to send us confidential comments on the working of the Act, particularly with regard to illegal abortions. Further, our secretary and medical secretary visited the United States and reported to us in writing on abortion in some of the States. We were not an idle Committee.

All the members had important work of their own to do and the way in which they managed so faithfully to attend the meetings was admirable. I remember one consultant coming at top speed from the operating theatre with hair still wet from being under the cap worn in the hot theatre. Another member was absent for a surprisingly short time after her baby was born. Two members lived in Scotland and had long travelling to do. Attendance at the meetings involved their colleagues or partners having extra work put on them, but I never heard of any of them complaining.

As to my own position, it was possible to arrange for some of the meetings, particularly the longer ones, to take place in the legal vacations. Otherwise I had to take days off from court. This may have sometimes resulted in my brethren having rather heavier lists, but mainly the work just had to be held up. Out of court hours I was able to do such things as settling the agenda for the next meeting and preparing the Report with the aid of the secretary's minutes. My own clerk typed out what I wrote and helped me as much as she could. I wrote the whole of Volume 1 of the Report myself, except for the historical notes. The general history of abortion, which is known to have been practised from pre-historic times, was written by my husband, Randall, and the history in Scotland by the Scottish Q.C. member. I could not possibly have found time to do the necessary research, the visits to libraries, the British Museum and so on which Randall undertook. He had retired and I think quite enjoyed it. I wanted to have the attribution in the Report but Randall would not allow it so the only people who were told at the time were the Committee members who were sworn to secrecy. So I got the credit for the history which was not my due but I see no reason now why Randall should not have it posthumously.

Volume II was the statistical Report and was entirely compiled and written by the government statisticians who assisted us and supplied us with tables and graphs during our deliberations.

Volume III contains the survey by the Institute for Social Studies in Medical Care.

After we had submitted the report in November 1973 there was a long hold-up in Stationery Office printing and it was not published until about January or February of the following year.

At the end of our labours I suggested that the Department might stand us a celebratory dinner. This was agreed and a modest establishment suggested as the venue. I was not going to have that and insisted that it must be in a private room at the Savoy Hotel. Not without demur, this was accepted. The hotel had stipulated that the menu must be its decision (because of the price being charged I suppose). We had a champagne party in the Temple flat first. It had seemed to me that it would give great pleasure to the Committee members if the Secretary of State himself could come to the party, but his secretary feared that his engagements would not permit it, particularly as he had to be somewhere well away from London during the afternoon of the day of the party. However, he arrived, I have no doubt at considerable personal inconvenience, and spent quite a long time with us and spoke to all the members individually. They were delighted and felt that their long efforts had been appreciated.

Afterwards we were safely conveyed in a Minibus to the Savoy Hotel where we had a most excellent dinner and a festive evening. There were speeches and to my surprised pleasure the members presented me with a Victorian gold brooch set with diamonds and a silver-gilt miniature match box. I cherish them along with the extraordinarily kind letters the members wrote to me individually.

Particularly having regard to the nature of our enquiry and the very strong emotions which may be aroused on the subject of abortion, we were a most harmonious and happy Committee with reasonable discussion, free from the acrimonious arguments which I understand sometimes do occur in committees. At any rate, our conclusions and report were unanimous.

It had been my impression that the government would incorporate at any rate some of our recommendations in a Bill to be put before Parliament, but before that could happen there was a general election, a different party was returned to power and there was no such Bill. The DHSS was able to give effect to a few of the recommendations under their own existing powers and I notice that public reference is still sometimes made to the Report.

When it was all over I was glad to have been able to do it but also happy to devote the whole of my time to judicial work and to return to uninterrupted daily contact at lunch and other times with my fellow Benchers, something of which I never tired.

When I was appointed it occurred to me that disapproval of a woman judge might be expressed by some newspaper writers or others: so far as I know there was none. By 1962 there was general sympathy for women being appointed to many offices traditionally held by men.

Nevertheless, for nine years I was the only woman High Court judge and then, to my joy, Mrs Justice Heilbron was appointed to the Family Division. On my retirement Mrs Justice Booth was similarly appointed and shortly afterwards so was Mrs Justice Butler-Sloss. So now there are three. Very good. Several women were appointed as Circuit judges before and after I retired.

Farewell

When it came to my final sitting in December 1978 I expected that perhaps up to a dozen members of the Bar would be present in court to say good-bye. I could not believe my eyes when I entered my very large Court. It was packed tight and people filled the aisles. Not only barristers but solicitors, social workers, court officials, and members of the public were squeezed in. My usher told me that there had almost been fighting in the corridor to get inside and that a lot of people had failed to do so. Standing on the Bench beside my chair was a member of the Court of Appeal, unrobed because otherwise he would have taken precedence and had to sit in my chair – which would have rather spoilt the effect.

There were valedictory speeches, which is usual when a judge is retiring, but I was so moved by all the kindness, that for the first time in court, I had difficulty in maintaining my composure and only just managed to keep my voice steady when I expressed my thanks and said my own farewell. It was a wonderful send-off which will always remain a very proud memory.

Chapter 11

Some other judges

There is an unbreakable tradition that a judge even after retirement does not comment publicly on any other living judge. But death lifts the ban and there are several deceased judges about whom I wish to say something. First let me remark on what a lamentably high number of judges have died while still quite young. Heart failure has carried off too many of them when they should have had many more years of work before them. There is no doubt that the judicial life is a hard one. People who think that judges have an easy time of it, sitting in court for only about five hours a day, have little idea of what long hours of work have to be done outside court hours. Perhaps the fact that judicial life may follow a very hard-working career at the Bar has something to do with the early deaths. A lot of judges can withstand the pressure of course, and live after retirement to a very old age.

Daniel Brabin and Eric Blain of the Queen's Bench Division, James Stirling of the Family Division and Reginald Goff of the Chancery Division all died from heart failure: Geoffrey Veale, John Cobb, Samuel Cooke and Raymond Hinchcliffe all of the Queen's Bench Division died from other causes. Only the last of these was near to retirement. Other judges were appointed to take their places but, for me, the death of each of them left a gap which could not be filled. Their obituaries have been written and it is not for me to write additional ones, but I hope that a few personal comments about them may be permissible.

Mr Justice Brabin

Danny Brabin was a Lancashire man and full of common sense. He was a most amusing companion and it was a delight to be out on Circuit with him. He was a strict teetotaller but at a party (which was something he loved) he became quite excited and his face became more and more flushed. Anyone who did not know that he drank nothing stronger than orange juice might have thought that he had consumed quiet a quantity of alcohol. On one occasion when we were both sitting at Cardiff and Randall came to spend the week-end with me, I wanted to show him Caerphilly Castle and Danny, who was going home by train for the week-end, lent me his car for the purpose. We drove round and round Caerphilly but could find nowhere to park within reasonable distance of the Castle. Finally, in desperation I parked in the fore-court of a bookmakers' premises. Nobody would have known whose car it was except that a police officer might well have spotted the number of the car as being Danny's. I confessed to him afterwards what I had done but so far from being annoyed, he roared with laughter.

Mr Justice Veale

Geoffrey Veale was an excellent judge, always courteous and gentle towards counsel and litigants alike. He loved his work dearly and when he was on Circuit not long before he died and his heart was giving trouble the doctor forbade him to go to court, he stood at the window to watch the judicial cars leaving for court, and the look on his face made plain his sad yearning to be going too.

157

Mr Justice Blain

Eric Blain was a charming and witty man as well as a good judge. He had a suavity which was completely disarming. I do not suppose that anyone was ever rude to him.

Mr Justice Stirling

James Stirling was a charmer and superb amateur actor. He was of rather short stature so that the stage parts he could have played were somewhat restricted. Otherwise I rather doubt whether the Law would have claimed him. I saw him in amateur productions of the Bar Theatrical Society and he gave the most polished and professional performances. Like Eric Blain he died on Circuit and in bed. Judges do not die in court as a rule: it would be too inconsiderate. James Stirling was found dead the morning after he had been a guest at a Circuit dinner and given, I was told, one of the best speeches the Circuit had ever heard.

Lord Justice Goff

Reginald Goff, as a member of the Chancery Division and later of the Court of Appeal, did not go on Circuit so I saw less of him than of the others I mention, but we always got on very well together when we did meet. I rather lost my heart to him in the year when we were appointed to the High Court. We both attended the Lord Chancellor's 'Breakfast' following the annual legal service in Westminster Abbey. He was about my height (I am not very tall) and had a very fresh complexion. He told me with obvious relish that a distinguished non-legal woman guest came up to him and said "I have been so anxious to meet you. You must be Mrs Justice Lane."

Full-bottomed wigs do make quite a good disguise, but how many men would have been so amused by the incident and recounted it as he did?

Mr Justice Cobb

John Cobb Q.C. was a member of the North-Eastern Circuit and sometimes appeared before me as counsel when I was sitting on the Circuit. He did his work splendidly and it seemed to me that he had the word 'Judge' written all over him, so it was no surprise when in 1975 he was so appointed. I had the good fortune to go on Circuit with him soon afterwards. By common consent it was immediately apparent that he made an excellent judge and should have had a fine judicial career. But, cruelly, in 1977 he died at the age of 55. He was a very real loss to the Bench and to his many friends.

Mr Justice Cooke

Samuel Cooke was another man loved by everyone who knew him. He was one of the kindest men I have ever met. Personally, I was very sorry when in 1973 he accepted the Chairmanship of the Law Commission. This is a very important post which no doubt he filled admirably, but I felt that he was too great a loss to the work of the courts and I bemoaned the fact that he no longer went on Circuit where I might hope to join him.

Mr Justice Hinchcliffe and Lady Hinchcliffe

Raymond Hinchcliffe and his wife, Poppy, were two of my dearest friends. He was a Yorkshireman and liked sitting at Leeds. This was not one of my favourite places on Circuit but I always tried to get there if Ray was going to be there. Poppy was nearly always with him. She was full of charm, kindness and grace. After Ray died Randall and I stayed with Poppy in the delightful house they had built in Yorkshire with a view to his retirement in 1975. Although he was able to go there he was already a sick man and died there not long afterwards.

After Randall died in 1975 it was to Poppy that I went once I could manage to travel. She helped me as no one else could have done. One day she said that she had arranged for us both to lunch with John Cobb and his wife. I protested that I could not possibly face it but she insisted and that marked the beginning of my return to normal life. I stayed with her again and saw her in London, but alas! she too died. I do not cease to miss both of them. As to Ray, he was a shrewd judge: it would have been difficult to pull the wool over his eyes. It was curious that he and I were so different and yet we thought alike on virtually every topic. We often discussed the cases each of us was trying and always reach the same conclusion. Ray hated injustice: he did not just deplore it as others might, he had a deep hatred for it. If something unjust had happened in a court or elsewhere Ray might get quite het up about it and almost bellow "That's *wrong!*" Yet he could feel sympathy for a wrongdoer. I remember his acute distress when he was trying an excellent police officer and realised that there must be a conviction and that he must impose a heavy sentence, though the victim of the offence was a worthless man for whom it was impossible to feel any real sympathy. This was not the only sentence which he regretted having to pass and is something which other judges may experience. On one occasion I told Ray that I had not met with the courtesy due to a judge from a member of the Bar, not in court, elsewhere. Ray was furious (that was *wrong*) and ordered the offending barrister to attend at the Lodgings the next day. I was not present at the interview of course, but I would not have liked to be in that man's shoes. I received a prompt and adequate letter of apology (and that was *right*).

160

Other judges died during my tenure of office and afterwards but I do not refer to them either because I cannot claim that they were particular friends of mine or because I have earlier made plain my admiration for them. But lest it be thought that what I have written is a too uncritical eulogy of judges, let me add that there were three judges whom I strongly disliked, one of whom I thoroughly despised. Although they are all dead, it seems unnecessary to refer to them by name.

Lord Goddard

There is yet one other judge about whom I will write and who became a dear friend of mine after his retirement and my becoming a Bencher of the same Inn of Court. I refer to the late Lord Goddard, a judge of the High Court in 1928, thereafter a Lord Justice of Appeal, later a Lord of Appeal and finally Lord Chief Justice from 1946 to 1958, when he retired. I know that he was regarded in some circles as a hard and unmerciful judge. In my view he was nothing of the sort. After he died in 1971 at the age of 94, there was an article about him in a well-known daily newspaper which was so adversely, and as I thought, unfairly critical of him that I was furious and vowed that I would never read another word the author wrote and I never have done.

I always found Lord Goddard fair and reasonable both in cases in which I appeared before him and others which were reported. It was said of him that he jumped to conclusions early in cases he was hearing. So he did, and his conclusions were usually right – not always though. But if he had initially got it wrong, there was no judge readier than he to admit it. If you were appearing before him and felt that your case deserved a different conclusion, you had to stick to your guns in the certain knowledge that he would listen carefully to your argument, give it due consideration and come round to the opposite of his first view if your case merited it. He would unhesitatingly say in terms that his first impression had been wrong, without any attempt to disguise the change of view.

As to harshness in sentencing, in my experience at least, he never passed a severe sentence unless it was deserved. It has to be remembered that times change and that sentences which may seem harsh in one period did not seem so in earlier times. After all it was not until 1832 that housebreaking, horsestealing, sheepstealing and coining ceased to be capital offences, or until after 1861 that no-one was hanged for any offence except murder or attempted murder. Transportation had been substituted as a 'merciful' alternative to the death penalty for felony in a series of statutes dating from the reign of Charles II. It was not finally abolished (because the Australian colonies and Tasmania refused to accept any more convicts) and penal servitude substituted until 1868, which was only nine years before Lord Goddard was born. He grew up in an era which had not long ceased to regard criminals as a nuisance to be got rid of and forgotten. But by the time he was called to the Bar ideas had been changing fast on many subjects including crime and no doubt he shared the horror felt for the inhumanity of earlier generations in their treatment of criminals. Nevertheless, in his later days, Lord Goddard shared the view held by many people much younger than he that too much emphasis was being placed on the welfare of the offender and too little on that of the victim. And I think that, in common with many other people inside and outside the legal profession, he was disappointed that no really effective means had been found of reforming criminals, particularly young ones. Again in common with many others, he did not, I think, entertain high hopes for the success of e g Borstal Training. He shared the still widely held view (to which I subscribe) that sentencing policy should be firmly based on retribution. An offender should get what he deserves, not excluding another chance if it is merited.

The problem is, of course, to determine what he deserves. It is interesting that, so far as I can tell, any recent public criticism of sentences passed has mainly been to the effect that they have been too lenient. Curiously, disloyalty and breach of trust has been the only example I can recall of complaints of excessive severity. But I do not pretend to have made a study of the subject and I am open to contradiction by those who know better.

It would be wrong to say that Lord Goddard was lacking in sympathy or understanding but if he saw his duty as including severe punishment for wrongdoers, I cannot see that this deserves criticism.

His work was not exclusively in the criminal field of course and as an instance of his sympathy and understanding in a civil case, I refer to one which was concerned with wartime and post-war regulations relating to the repair of war-damaged properties. To the best of my recollection the facts were these: a pharmaceutical chemist occupied leased shop premises where his father had carried on the same business before him. The premises were damaged in an air-raid, not sufficiently to oblige him to shut up shop, but certainly severely enough to necessitate substantial repairs. In accordance with statutory requirements the landlords served a first notice on him to which he duly responded, then a further notice which required a counter-notice which he failed to give. In consequence the landlords were entitled to require him to give up his tenancy and to possession of the shop. I was briefed for the landlords to seek an order to this effect. I felt sorry for the chemist, but there seemed to be no answer to the claim. At the hearing he was not represented and appeared not to understand what had happened to him. I knew that Lord Goddard, who was to hear the application, would not be pleased with it. I opened my case by saying "My Lord I have no merits but in my submission, as your Lordship will find, technically my clients are within their rights." It was then necessary to wade through the relevant Regulations. At the end

Lord Goddard gave a meticulously accurate judgment referring to the various relevant paragraphs of the Regulations and, inevitably, found for the landlords. The poor little chemist sat there looking more bewildered than ever. Lord Goddard then said to him words to this effect: "You cannot have been able to follow the technicalities of the judgment I have just given so I will now explain to you in simple language which you can understand why you have lost your shop." It left the chemist no less sorrowful but at least he then understood why he was being turned out.

When I was first made a Bencher I was somewhat apprehensive as to whether Lord Goddard might resent the advent of a woman to that long-hallowed male preserve. He knew me from my appearances before him and never seemed to be displeased with my work, but to be a fellow-Bencher was something different altogether. Shortly after the event I met him: he looked me up and down and said "Good morning – Dame." The pause was eloquent, so I answered "Good morning – Lord." Thereafter the ice began to melt and it was not long before we were on excellent terms. He had retired some seven years before I arrived on the scene, having remained at his post until he was about 81 years old. The rule as to compulsory retirement at 75 did not apply to him as it was not introduced until long after his appointment. He was still in good health when I was appointed, but as the years went by it began to fail and eventually he had to use a wheelchair. He much enjoyed coming to Sunday lunch at the Inn when Benchers may invite a guest (usually a spouse). But he began to tire before the party broke up so he would give me a signal to come and push him in his chair into another room. (Nobody else was allowed that privilege unless I was absent.) Arrived there he wished to be transferred to an arm chair and somehow I always managed to get him there, though I used to wonder whether with his great weight I should hear my spine crack! I was thankful that his manservant came to get him back into the wheelchair and take him home, but I was very happy to be able to do something useful for a man I greatly respected and for whom I had developed real affection. He died on 30 May 1971.

Lord Darling

Off the Bench Lord Goddard was a most interesting and amusing companion but he was not a judge who was remembered for his witticisms in Court. He was not like Lord Darling who is probably best remembered for his. For example:

Witness: "I got off at Elephant and Castle to make a telephone call."

Lord Darling: "A trunk call I presume."

The one I like is of a very young and nervous counsel who opened his case thus:

Counsel: "My Lord, my client is a Mrs Winterwoman who is a washerbottom."

Lord Darling: "What an odd profession. Hadn't you better call her a laundress?"

On occasion, intentionally or otherwise, Lord Darling gave counsel an opportunity to make a crack of his own. For instance:

Lord Darling: "Who is George Robey?"

Counsel: "My Lord he is the darling of the halls."

And in a case which concerned the Coliseum theatre:

Lord Darling: "The Coliseum? Isn't that the place where they throw Christians as food to the lions?"

Counsel: "Your Lordship is thinking of the Trocadero where Lyons throw food to the Christians."

There is another reason why lawyers at any rate may remember Lord Darling. In 1900 he was the victim of what must have been the most scurrilous libel ever published about a judge. A Birmingham newspaper editor perpetrated it, including this: "There is not a journalist in Birmingham who has anything to learn from the impudent little man in horsehair, a microcosm of conceit and empty-headedness."

A judge does not defend himself by bringing a libel action. But the Attorney-General can, and in this case did, bring proceedings for Contempt of Court. The editor duly apologised (it must have nearly choked him!) and was not sent to prison but fined a modest £100 with £25 costs. In those days these were not really paltry sums but I suppose would hardly be noticed by the dailies of today, some of which offer to make a competitor-reader a rich man, if not a millionaire, in order to boost their circulation.

Judges do not expect to be treated as sacred and exempt from all criticism. Lord Atkin summed up the position in the House of Lords in these words:

"Justice is not a cloistered virtue. She must be allowed to suffer the scrutiny and respectful, even though outspoken, comments of ordinary man."★

★*Ambard v Attorney-General for Trinidad and Tobago* (1936).

Chapter 12

Some changes in the law and its observance

Now that I have virtually finished the account of my legal career it seems to me to be appropriate to refer to some changes in the law in recent times, to some developments in it which I would like to see and also to some novel instances of illegality.

Freedom and the law

In our fundamental dislike of what we see as restrictions on our personal liberty we resemble the French or the Italians more than the Germans. But one way in which we do not resemble our European neighbours is in the ignorance of so many people about our legal system and the law it administers. This ignorance is perhaps less marked than it used to be because of the numerous television programmes showing court scenes. In the earlier ones which I watched there were often glaring inaccuracies in procedure and the presentation of evidence, but latterly the few which I have seen have been much better and given the impression that the producers and scriptwriters have come to rely less on imagination and more on expert advice. Nevertheless, I have found even poorly-educated French, Italians and Spanish more knowledgeable about their own law than is the case here. Perhaps that is because we are more law-abiding and so have less occasion to learn!

167

However, it must be said that English law changes so rapidly that lawyers themselves have difficulty in keeping up with it. One of the most frightening sights I ever saw was just after the last war: the huge room at the Stationery Office which housed the Statutory Instruments (made under Acts of Parliament). Row upon row of them right around the walls. I did not count even the files holding them, but if the Instruments did not run into millions there must have been many thousands. I fled!

The purpose of law is to protect the freedom of the subject. Paradoxically this can only be achieved by restricting the freedom of some in favour of others. If one man is to be free from attack by another, the other cannot be free to attack the one. The more complicated society becomes the more restrictions are found to be necssary. The aim of much modern legislation has been to protect the weak against the strong. For example, freedom of contract has been whittled down. The old rule in contract was *caveat emptor* (let the buyer beware) but now the buyer has all kinds of protection, for instance in hire-purchase contracts, landlord and tenant contracts, contracts containing unfair terms, contracts of employment, and so on. Trades union law was originally intended to protect the weak employee against the strong employer, but it seems to me that nowadays the public needs protection against at any rate the public service unions. The principle that just as a man has a right to work at his job, so a man has a right to withhold his labour surely needs modification in the nationalised industries and other public services. In my view strikes in those services have become all too like blackmail, with the public as the victim. I would make all such strikes illegal, just as they are in the armed services. Such a measure would of course be met with howls of rage and perhaps, initially at any rate, strikes which would have to be dealt with punitively if reason failed.

In place of strikes

How then could employees in the public services be protected from inadequate wages and unsatisfactory conditions of work? The controlling bodies of public services are, in the main, composed of reasonably fair-minded men, but lest tyranny raise its ugly head among them, I would suggest that, perhaps with a right of appeal to the Court of Appeal and thence to the House of Lords on points of law, tribunals could be set up to which unions could appeal. There are already Employment Tribunals with their own Appeal Tribunals which decide between a man and his employer in cases of dismissal. A main difficulty with the tribunals I am suggesting would probably be the selection of those to sit on them. If the choice were left to the government of the day it might be disastrous and the members might change from right to left with each party in power because I do not think that membership could be until a set retiring age, it would have to be for a fixed period of time. A joint Parliamentary selection committee might be a solution: candidates could be proposed to the committee by the governing bodies of industries and services to which the strike ban applied and by officers of the unions concerned. Past or present members of those governing bodies and past or present holders of office in those unions would have to be ineligible. These are tentative ideas and no doubt better ones can be devised. For all I know the Government has already done this. I firmly believe that a cessation of strikes in the nationalised industries and public services has become indispensable to the welfare of the country. After all, the total membership of trades unions amounts to only a minority of the whole population and it is undemocratic that they should seek to impose their will on the majority. This is not to deny the duty of the majority to provide adequate protection for minority rights and interest. Neither is it to deny that the aim of the law should be to protect the weak against the strong. Power cuts which leave people in cold and darkness; public transport strikes which leave people helplessly stranded and unable to travel to and from work or for many other purposes including holidays; strikes which deprive members of other unions or even the strikers' own of their right to work and so forth; and teachers who penalise children, all these demonstrate clearly which are the weak who are made to suffer and which are the strong who are able to impose such hardships.

Legal aid

In a very different sphere in which the law seeks to protect the weak against the strong I refer to legal aid in civil litigation. (I have nothing to say about legal aid in criminal prosecutions: this is obviously right, although I wish that some means could be found of limiting unnecessary extravagance in the process.) This aim has been achieved in a great number of civil cases but at the same time it has caused real hardship and unfairness to many of those who have been outside its provisions. In the preamble to the Legal Aid and Advice Act 1949 (since repealed and replaced) those who were to benefit from its provisions were 'persons of small or moderate means'. The term was in effect defined by the limits set on the means of those who were entitled to benefit. These limits were increased by subsequent legislation but, allowing for the contributions towards his costs which a legally aided party is required to make, the result has been to put him in the position of a person of superabundant means. Whereas the other party may not be able to afford, eg costly expert evidence or bringing witnesses from abroad. Any person or body with adequate means to litigate nevertheless weighs the anticipated gain to be derived against the costs of bringing or defending an action. Not infrequently it is not worth while doing so.

Not so the legally aided litigant. True the legally aided litigant who is successful (as he is in the majority of cases) must repay his costs to the legal aid fund out of the gain he makes, but in many cases this may not be sufficient to cover his costs in full, so the State may pay the whole or part of the costs of an action which an unaided litigant would not have considered worth while bringing or defending. Further, the threat of being met by a legally aided party may force a man into settling a claim, even when he believes he has a good case, because he cannot afford to fight a costly action.

One of the worst injustices caused by the legal aid legislation is in the matter of costs. When the 1949 Act was passed I read it, was puzzled, thought I had missed something and read it again. But I had not missed it, there was no provision for the payment of costs out of the Fund to a successful unaided party. This seemed to me to be a 'heads I win, tails you lose' situation and plainly unfair. An order could be made against the legally aided party personally but this was usually limited to the amount of his contribution to his own costs, which might be nil. This was not an entirely new situation: before the Act was passed a claim might be brought by a plaintiff of little or no substance so that if the defendant were successful he had virtually no hope of recovering his costs, but before the Act such cases were comparatively rare. Since the Act they have multiplied. As a result the courts were sometimes reduced to making an order for costs against an unsuccessful legally aided party 'not to be enforced without further leave of the Court.' This was in the forlorn hope that the party might subsequently make or inherit money, or win a football pool or the like. I never heard of such leave being applied for, let alone granted. It was not until 15 years later that this injustice was partially remedied. By the Legal Act Act 1964 (since repealed and replaced) an unaided successful defendant who had not instigated the proceedings could receive the whole or any part of his costs out of the legal aid fund but even then

171

only if it was 'just and equitable' for him to do so and if 'the unassisted party will suffer severe financial hardship unless the order is made'.

In my respectful opinion, the laudable desire of Parliament to protect public funds can occasionally go rather too far. Nobody need shed tears over the situation of wealthy corporations or private individuals well able to afford their costs of success, although in effect this amounts to additional taxation, but there were and still are numerous cases where the less wealthy did and do suffer real hardship even though the courts cannot hold it to be 'severe'. To begin with the courts were very strict in their interpretation of that word, although as the years have gone by, and particularly since the original provision was re-enacted by the Legal Aid Act 1974, there has been a tendency for a somewhat less strict interpretation. There is, however, one more hurdle for the successful unassisted litigant to surmount: at the conclusion of a hearing the court cannot then and there make an order for payment out of the legal aid fund, but must adjourn the application for costs to a Master or Registrar for enquiry and report. The appropriate committee of the Law Society may then oppose such an order being made. Sometimes this procedure may be obviated by the committee, whose members are sensible people, giving advance notification that an order for costs out of the fund will not be opposed. This saves time and further costs.

How difficult it is to do good by Act of Parliament without also doing harm!

There is one way in which the inequalities created by the legal aid legislation could be lessened, even though not removed, which is not my own idea but emanates from more eminent sources. The suggestion is that the present restrictions on eligibility for legal aid should be abolished altogether and, instead, there should be a sliding scale of contributions based not only on the means of the applicant for legal aid but also on the likely costs of the litigation. The result would be that people with abundant means would not even apply but those with more moderate means who could afford the costs of a simple action but not of long and costly proceedings would be able to enforce or defend their legal rights. In short, the tests would be whether the applicant could reasonably afford the contemplated litigation out of his own resources. This reform would cost money and legal aid costs the taxpayer millions already, but if justice so requires, so be it. Some of the additional money could be found by raising the present rate of contributions to a more realistic level. Then if the legally aided litigant wins all well and good, he recovers his contributions and if he loses it is because he did not have a good case.

Anti-ism

I refer next to something which is new in my lifetime and which quite frequently leads to offences being committed but which I do not think can be dealt with other than by existing law.

This is what I can only call 'anti-ism'. This word is not in the dictionary but new phenomena need new words. By it I mean being against something for the sake of being against something, no matter what.

The suffragettes were *for* something – the right to vote. The C.N.D. declares itself to be for nuclear disarmament but, in my view, it is better described as being against nuclear arms. There cannot be any sane person in the West who is not whole-heartedly against their use and if the Soviet Union would show itself more amenable to reason the entirety of the hideous weapons could gradually be destroyed. But the governments of the West have to face reality and the reality is that this splendid aim has hitherto been impossible of achievement, therefore it is their duty to be able to defend their countries. The only feasible way to do this is by having sufficient like weapons for retaliation in kind and thus to deter the other side from using theirs. Does anyone really believe that atom bombs would have been dropped on Nagasaki and Hiroshima if the Japanese had had nuclear weapons of their own? The answer seems to me to be plain as a pikestaff and it is 'no'. If the C.N.D. were able to influence the Soviet Union towards abandoning nuclear arms, no doubt we should all be for it but I cannot understand how anyone can believe that the C.N.D. can do otherwise than encourage the Soviets to maintain or increase their supply of nuclear arms in the hope or belief that the campaign will influence the government to reduce or abandon our nuclear arms and thus make us into sitting ducks. It must be the case that a great number of C.N.D. members are sincere and well-meaning people, but why should they consider themselves wiser than their governments in the matter of national defence? And how can they consider themselves justified in their futile attempts to influence their govenments, in England at any rate, by using such means as committing criminal damage to property and making an unhygienic nuisance of themselves to the neighbourhood of their squalid camps? It is largely because of the way in which the campaign is conducted that I draw the conclusion that a good many of the members are simply gratifying their desire to be against something.

In a different sphere, I have more sympathy for anti-abortionists, although I disagree with them. Some of them may be tainted with 'anti-ism', but from what I have seen it is probable that the majority are activated by religious and moral scruples. At least they do not besiege hospitals or burst into operating theatres to try to stop abortion being carried out.

Another of the 'anti-' campaigns seems to me to have no validity at all, namely the 'Animal Liberation Front'. In order to protect the fox, they are prepared to injure horses and hounds and to go hooded to attack their fellow-humans. I do not think that I am less mindful of

174

the welfare of animals than most people but we have a very efficeint and dedicated Royal Society for the Prevention of Cruelty to Animals, and law for the protection of animals and birds. A campaign to raise money for the R.S.P.C.A. would deserve and receive support, although I believe that this excellent body is now in danger of being 'infiltrated' by extremist members of the A.L.F. If this is allowed to happen and the R.S.P.C.A. is thereby influenced towards the use of violent or otherwise illegal means of achieving its objects, the result of course would be that it would lose the sympathy and support of many if not most of its supporters and thus defeat its own ends.

If people consider hunting or fishing to be wrong, they need not take part in either, but they have no right whatsoever to interfere with other people's sporting interests. And if they wish to be vegetarians that is their business but the vast majority of people here prefer and thrive on their normal diet which includes meat and fish.

As for experiments on live animals, the Anti-Vivisection Society ran a well-conducted campaign which probably influenced and continues to influence Parliament in enacting strict controls of research on live animals of all kinds including vermin such as rats and mice. But the kind of outrageous behaviour which we have witnessed recently with premises being broken into, equipment damaged and animals 'freed' seems to me to be indefensible. Subject to the appropriate controls such research seems to be acceptable to most people for the purpose of reducing human ills.

As to false or real threats to poison sweets or other foods or throwing a petrol bomb so as to frighten or injure people, these are not only unlawful but completely despicable. This is surely terrorism at its cowardly worst. Such conduct is also futile and self-defeating in that it antagonises everybody else. If the 'liberationists' cannot see that for themselves, then I suppose that nothing will get it into their stupid heads. The desecration of the grave of the late Duke of Beaufort because he had been a hunting man and a Master of foxhonds when they could no longer hurt him was the act of loathsome ghouls.

All these doings of the A.L.F. reinforce my view that at any rate many of its members have no altruistic aims but have only the spite and destructiveness which characterises 'anti-ism'. If there are sincere and reasonable members of the organisation it is unfortunate but inevitable that they should be tarred with the same brush.

What, I wonder, will the 'anti-ists' campaign for next – the protection of slugs against gardeners, or the liberation of performing fleas (if there are any left)? I cannot think of any but a ridiculous suggestion to make.

Final thoughts

Whatever criticisms may be made of the law of this country, I believe, as I always have done, that it is the best and fairest system in the world, even if its Statutes are not always couched in language of sparkling clarity.

The probability seems to me to be that the law will grow ever more complex as new situations arise which require statutory regulation. A considerable amount of revision and re-enactment in one statute instead of in several would desirably simplify even its present complexity.

As long as we have laws there will, I suppose, be law-breakers as there always have been in historical times. Perhaps if it were otherwise a good many of those who make a career in the law would be made redundant. Until that day, no doubt they will continue to perform a necessary and valuable service.

Chapter 13

In retirement – but not quite

Finally I return to my personal story and come to my last chapter.

In August 1975 Randall died. He was in hospital for less than three weeks during which he underwent two operations, but his life could not be saved. In another five months we should have celebrated our golden wedding. If it had not been for the affectionate care and encouragement of my brother and of my friends I do not think that I could have managed to get back to my judicial duties by the beginning of the October term. Once I did so, it was a great help to have absorbing work to do.

Before Randall died we had been looking for a house where we could live when I retired, as he had done some years earlier. For a couple of years after his death I did not bother to re-start the search, but then it seemed that the matter must be taken in hand. It took over a year before I found and bought my present house. It stood empty for several months until I retired in January 1979, some 18 months before reaching the compulsory retirement age of seventy-five. Until after the last war there had been no retirement age for judges. Several of them who had been on the Bench when I was appointed stayed on until they were well over that age, for happy examples, Lord Denning and Mr Justice Stable.

It was painfully plain that it would be a great wrench to leave the life I had loved and the fine residential chambers in the Temple where Randall and I had been so happy.

But, for various reasons, I did not wish to stay on in the Temple after I retired and it seemed wise to make the break while I still had plenty of energy left to start a different kind of life.

It took the best part of a year to get the house as I wanted it and to settle down with, as I thought, my working life behind me. But in January 1980 I was invited to sit as an additional member of the Court of Appeal. Thereafter, for periods of between a week and a month I continued to do so when required for two and a half years. Different Lords Justices presided over the courts in which I sat. Most of the appeals were on matters of which I had had experience but, for the first time, I had to learn some of the intricacies of the Immigration Acts and some of the Employment Acts. It was all extemely interesting and very hard work. I loved it.

Thanks to the kindness of friends, I was able to stay in the Temple when I was sitting. It was rather strange to find myself once more treading the way I knew so well between the Temple and the Law Courts. At first, I felt somewhat posthumous. It was a delight to be again with the judges and the Benchers of my Inn and to 'talk shop'.

When Lord Denning retired in July 1982, the new Master of the Rolls made certain changes in the organisation of the Court of Appeal. I was not invited to sit again. This suited me very well because by then I was beginning to find the work rather too tiring and had decided not to sit again. But I was saved from having to refuse, which I should have been unhappy to do. I had sat in the Court of Appeal on several occasions while I was a judge, but I had never wanted promotion to that Court because for day-in-day-out work I preferred dealing with human beings to being concerned with problems on paper. It was, however, a remarkable experience to sit there and I would not have missed it for anything in the world.

One other honour came my way which gave me great pleasure: I was made an honorary member of the Western

Circuit. As such I could, and still do, attend some of the Circuit dinners among Circuit judges and members of the Bar, where I still feel very much at home.

Winchester is a delightful city and I know of no other place where I would prefer to live. There are Judges' Lodgings and it is a joy to dine there as I do quite frequently. By great good fortune, there are two families who are very close neighbours and are charming and kindness itself. If ever I need a helping hand, it is always available. They have become dear friends.★ I also have other friends in Winchester and have no need to feel lonely, but I am beginning to feel rather antique and am content to be quietly at home, without too much entertainment.

Delightful though it was to live in the Temple with its large and beautiful garden, I always had a slight hankering for a garden of my own. Now that I have one I find that I am not a very good or clever gardener. But I derive much pleasure from what I do achieve with the help of a gardener at times.

Looking back, the deep sorrow over my son and the death of Randall were the two great tragedies of my life. In every other way I have been exceptionally fortunate and have led an extremely interesting and privileged life. I have met with much kindness and known deep happiness. I am duly thankful to the Almighty for what I have received.

★Postscription: one of the families has moved since I wrote the foregoing, but only five miles away, so we have not lost touch.

Index

Index